AF560632

# HANDBOOK OF DAIRY PRODUCTS

# HANDBOOK OF DAIRY PRODUCTS

*By*

**Dr. Ashok Kumar**

*Deptt. of Zoology*
*Bundelkhand University*
*Campus Department*
*Jhansi*
*(India)*

**DISCOVERY PUBLISHING HOUSE PVT. LTD.**
**NEW DELHI-110 002**

*Published by:*
**Tilak Wasan**

**DISCOVERY PUBLISHING HOUSE PVT. LTD.**
4383/4A, Ansari Road, Darya Ganj
New Delhi-110 002 (India)
*Phone* : +91-11-23279245, 43596064-65
*Fax* : +91-11-23253475
*E-mail* : parul.wasan@gmail.com
discoverypublishinghouse@gmail.com
*web* : www.discoverypublishinggroup.com

***First Edition:* 2012**
**ISBN: 978-93-5056-006-8**

*Handbook of Dairy Products*


***Printed at:***
***Shree Balaji Art Press***
***Delhi***

# Preface

Dairy products are generally defined as foods produced from Cow's or Domestic Buffalo's milk. They are usually high-energy-yielding food products. A production plant for such processing is called a dairy or a dairy factory. Raw milk for processing mostly comes from Cows and to a lesser amount from Domestic Buffalos , but occasionally from other mammals such as goats, sheep, yaks, or horses. Dairy products are commonly found in European, Middle Eastern and Indian cuisine, whereas they are almost unknown in East Asian cuisine.

A dairy is a facility for the extraction and processing of animal milk — mostly from cows or goats, but also from buffalo, sheep, horses or camels — for human consumption. Typically it is a farm(*dairy farm*) or section of a farm that is concerned with the production of milk, butter and cheese.

In the more recent past, people in agricultural societies owned dairy animals that they milked for domestic and local (village) consumption, a typical example of a cottage industry. The animals might serve multiple purposes (for example, as a draught animal for pulling a plough as a youngster, and at the end of its useful life as meat). In this case the animals were normally milked by hand and the herd size was quite small, so that all of the animals could be milked in less than an hour — about 10 per milker. These tasks were performed by a *dairymaid* (*dairywoman*) or *dairyman*. The word *dairy* harkens back to Middle English *dayerie, deyerie,* from *deye* (female servant or dairymaid) and further back to Old English *dæge* (kneader of bread).

With industrialisation and urbanisation, the supply of milk became a commercial industry, with specialised breeds of cattle being developed for dairy, as distinct from beef or draught animals. Initially, more people were employed as milkers, but it soon turned to mechanisation with machines designed to do the milking.

Historically, the milking and the processing took place close together in space and time: on a dairy farm. People milked the animals by hand; on farms where only small numbers are kept, hand-milking may still be practiced. Hand-milking is accomplished by grasping the teats (often pronounced *tit* or *tits*) in the hand and expressing milk either by squeezing the fingers progressively, from the udder end to the tip, or by squeezing the teat between thumb and index finger, then moving the hand downward from udder towards the end of the teat. The action of the hand or fingers is designed to close off the milk duct at the udder (upper) end and, by the movement of the fingers, close the duct progressively to the tip to express the trapped milk. Each half or quarter of the udder is emptied one milk-duct capacity at a time.

Dairy may cause health issues for individuals with lactose intolerance and asthma etc. Dairy products may be contaminated with the fungus Aspergillus fumigatus which can cause asthma and other respiratory problems. Vegans and some vegetarians avoid dairy products due to a variety of ethical, dietary, environmental, political, and religious concerns.

**Author**

# Contents

1

# Introduction

Dairy products are generally defined as foods produced from Cow's or Domestic Buffalo's milk. They are usually high-energy-yielding food products. A production plant for such processing is called a dairy or a dairy factory. Raw milk for processing mostly comes from Cows and to a lesser amount from Domestic Buffalos, but occasionally from other mammals such as goats, sheep, yaks, or horses. Dairy products are commonly found in European, Middle Eastern and Indian cuisine, whereas they are almost unknown in East Asian cuisine.

**Types of Dairy Products**

Milk after optional homogenization, pasteurization, in several grades after standardization of the fat level, and possible addition of bacteria *Streptococcus lactis* and *Leuconostoc citrovorum.*

Crème fraîche, slightly fermented cream.

Smetana, Central and Eastern European variety of sour cream.

Clotted cream, thick spoonable cream made by heating.

Cultured buttermilk, fermented concentrated (water removed) milk using the same bacteria as sour cream.

Kefir, fermented milk resembling buttermilk but based on different yeast and bacteria culture.

Kumis/Airag, slightly fermented mares' milk popular in Central Asia.

Milk powder (or powdered milk), produced by removing the water from milk.

Whole milk products

Buttermilk products

Skim milk

Whey products

Ice Cream

High milk-fat and nutritional products (for infant formulas).

Cultured and confectionery products.

Condensed milk, milk which has been concentrated by evaporation, often with sugar added for longer life in an opened can.

Evaporated milk, (less concentrated than condensed) milk without added sugar.

Ricotta cheese, milk heated and reduced in volume, known in Indian cuisine as Khoa.

Infant formula, dried milk powder with specific additives for feeding human infants.

Baked milk, a variety of boiled milk that has been particularly popular in Russia.

Butter, mostly milk fat, produced by churning cream.

Buttermilk, the liquid left over after producing butter from cream, often dried as livestock food.

Ghee, clarified butter, by gentle heating of butter and removal of the solid matter.

Anhydrous milkfat.

Cheese, produced by coagulating milk, separating from whey and letting it ripen, generally with bacteria and sometimes also with certain molds.

Curds, the soft curdled part of milk (or skim milk) used to make cheese (or casein).

Whey, the liquid drained from curds and used for further processing or as a livestock food.

Cottage cheese.

Quark

Cream cheese, produced by the addition of cream to milk and then curdled to form a rich curd or cheese made from skim milk with cream added to the curd.

Fromage frais

Casein

Caseinates

Milk protein concentrates and isonates

Whey protein concentrates and isonates

Hydrolysates

Mineral concentrates

Yogurt, milk fermented by *Streptococcus salivarius ssp. thermophilus* and *Lactobacillus delbrueckii ssp. bulgaricus* sometimes with additional bacteria, such as *Lactobacillus acidophilus*.

Ayran

Lassi

Clabber (food), milk naturally fermented top yogurt-like state.

Gelato, slowly frozen milk and water, lesser fat than ice cream.

Ice cream, slowly frozen cream and emulsifying additives.

Ice milk

Frozen custard

Frozen yogurt, yogurt with emulsifiers that is frozen

Other

Viili

Kajmak

Filmjölk

Piimä

Vla

Dulce de leche

## Health Risks of Consuming Dairy Products

Dairy may cause health issues for individuals with lactose intolerance and asthma etc . Dairy products may be contaminated with the fungus Aspergillus fumigatus which can cause asthma and other respiratory problems. Vegans and some vegetarians avoid dairy products due to a variety of ethical, dietary, environmental, political, and religious concerns.

## Dairy

A dairy is a facility for the extraction and processing of animal milk — mostly from cows or goats, but also from buffalo, sheep, horses or camels — for human consumption. Typically it is a farm (*dairy farm*) or section of a farm that is concerned with the production of milk, butter and cheese.

Terminology differs slightly between countries. In particular, in the U.S. a *dairy* can also be a facility that processes, distributes and sells dairy products, or a room, building or establishment where milk is kept and butter or cheese is made. In New Zealand English a *dairy* means a corner convenience store, or Superette — and *dairy factory* is the term for what is elsewhere called a *dairy*.As an attributive, the word *dairy* refers to milk-based products, derivatives and processes, and the animals and workers involved in their production: for example dairy cattle, dairy goat. A dairy farm produces milk and a dairy factory processes it into a variety of dairy products. These establishments constitute the dairy industry, a component of the food industry.Milk producing animals have been domesticated for thousands of years. Initially, they were part of the subsistence farming that nomads engaged in. As the community moved about the country, their animals accompanied them. Protecting and feeding the animals were a big part of the symbiotic relationship between the animals and the herders.

In the more recent past, people in agricultural societies owned dairy animals that they milked for domestic and local (village) consumption, a typical example of a cottage industry. The animals might serve multiple purposes (for example, as a draught animal for pulling a plough as a youngster, and at the end of its useful life as meat). In this case the animals were normally milked by hand and the herd size was quite small, so that all of the animals could be milked in less than an hour — about 10 per milker. These tasks were performed by a *dairymaid* (*dairywoman*) or *dairyman*. The word *dairy* harkens back to Middle English *dayerie, deyerie,* from *deye* (female servant or dairymaid) and further back to Old English *dæge* (kneader of bread).

With industrialisation and urbanisation, the supply of milk became a commercial industry, with specialised breeds of cattle being developed for dairy, as distinct from beef or draught animals. Initially, more people were employed as milkers, but it soon turned to mechanisation with machines designed to do the milking.

Historically, the milking and the processing took place close together in space and time: on a dairy farm. People milked the animals by hand; on farms where only small numbers are kept, hand-milking may still be practiced. Hand-milking is accomplished by grasping the teats (often pronounced *tit* or *tits*) in the hand and expressing milk either by squeezing the fingers progressively, from the udder end to the tip, or by squeezing the teat between thumb and index finger, then moving the hand downward from udder towards the end of the teat. The action of the hand or fingers is designed to close off the milk duct at the udder (upper) end and, by the movement of the fingers, close the duct progressively to the tip to express the trapped milk. Each half or quarter of the udder is emptied one milk-duct capacity at a time.

The *stripping* action is repeated, using both hands for speed. Both methods result in the milk that was trapped in the milk duct being squirted out the end into a bucket that is supported between the knees (or rests on the ground) of the milker, who usually sits on a low stool.

Traditionally the cow, or cows, would stand in the field or paddock while being milked. Young stock, heifers, would have to be trained to remain still to be milked. In many countries, the cows were tethered to a post and milked. The problem with this method is that it relies on quiet, tractable beasts, because the hind end of the cow is not restrained.

In 1937, it was found that bovine somatotropin (bST or bovine growth hormone) would increase the yield of milk. Monsanto Company developed a synthetic (recombinant) version of this hormone (rBST). In February 1994, rBST was approved by the Food and Drug Administration (FDA) for use in the U.S. It has become common in the U.S., but not elsewhere, to inject it into milch kine (dairy cows) to increase their production by up to 15 per cent.

However, there are claims that this practice can have negative consequences for the animals themselves. A European Union scientific commission was asked to report on the incidence of mastitis and other disorders in dairy cows, and on other aspects of the welfare of dairy cows. The commission's statement, subsequently adopted by the European Union, stated that the use of rBST substantially increased health problems with cows, including foot problems, mastitis and injection site reactions, impinged on the welfare of the animals and caused reproductive disorders. The report concluded that on the basis of the health and welfare of the animals, rBST should not be used. Health Canada prohibited the sale of rBST in 1999; the recommendations of external committees were that, despite not finding a significant health risk to humans, the drug presented a threat to animal health and for this reason, could not be sold in Canada.

## Structure of the Industry

While most countries produce their own milk products, the structure of the dairy industry varies in different parts of the world. In major milk-producing countries most milk is distributed through wholesale markets. In Ireland and Australia, for example, farmers' co-operatives own many of the large-scale processors, while in the United States many farmers and processors do business through individual contracts. In the United States, the country's 196 farmers' cooperatives sold 86 per cent of milk in the U.S. in 2002, with five cooperatives accounting for half that. This was down from 2,300 cooperatives in the 1940s. In developing countries, the past practice of farmers marketing milk in their own neighbourhoods are changing rapidly. Notable developments include considerable foreign investment in the dairy industry and a growing role for dairy cooperatives. Output of milk is growing rapidly in such countries and presents a major source of income growth for many farmers.

As in many other branches of the food industry, dairy processing in the major dairy producing countries has become increasingly concentrated, with fewer but larger and more efficient plants operated by fewer workers. This is notably the case in the United States, Europe, Australia and New Zealand. In 2009, charges of anti-trust violations have been made against major dairy industry players in the United States.

Government intervention in milk markets was common in the 20th century. A limited anti-trust exemption was created for U.S. dairy cooperatives by the Capper-Volstead Act of 1922. In the 1930s, some U.S. states adopted price controls, and Federal Milk Marketing Orders started under the Agricultural Marketing Agreement Act of 1937 and continue in the 2000s. The Federal Milk Price Support Programme began in 1949. The Northeast Dairy Compact regulated wholesale milk prices in New England from 1997 to 2001.

Plants producing liquid milk and products with short shelf life, such as yogurts, creams and soft cheeses, tend to be located on the outskirts of urban centres close to consumer markets. Plants manufacturing items with longer shelf life, such as butter, milk powders, cheese and whey powders, tend to be situated in rural areas closer to the milk supply. Most large processing plants tend to specialise in a limited range of products. Exceptionally, however, large plants producing a wide range of products are still common in Eastern Europe, a holdover from the former centralized, supply-driven concept of the market.

As processing plants grow fewer and larger, they tend to acquire bigger, more automated and more efficient equipment. While this technological tendency keeps manufacturing costs lower, the need for long-distance transportation often increases the environmental impact.

Milk production is irregular, depending on cow biology. Producers must adjust the mix of milk which is sold in liquid form *vs*. processed foods (such as butter and cheese) depending on changing supply and demand.

## Operation of the Dairy Farm

When it became necessary to milk larger numbers of cows, the cows would be brought to a shed or barn that was set up with bails (stalls) where the cows could be confined while they were milked. One person could milk more cows this way, as many as 20 for a skilled worker. But having cows standing about in the yard and shed waiting to be milked is not good for the cow, as she needs as much time in the paddock grazing as is possible. It is usual to restrict the twice-daily milking to a maximum of an hour and a half each time. It makes no difference whether one milks 10 or 1000 cows, the milking time should not exceed a total of about three hours each day for any cow.

As herd sizes increased there was more need to have efficient milking machines, sheds, milk-storage facilities (vats), bulk-milk transport and shed cleaning capabilities and the means of getting cows from paddock to shed and back.

Farmers found that cows would abandon their grazing area and walk towards the milking area when the time came for milking. This is not surprising as, in the flush of the milking season, cows presumably get very uncomfortable with udders engorged with milk, and the place of relief for them is the milking shed.

As herd numbers increased so did the problems of animal health. In New Zealand two approaches to this problem have been used. The first was improved veterinary medicines (and the government regulation of the medicines) that the farmer could use. The other was the creation of *veterinary clubs* where groups of farmers would employ a veterinarian (vet) full-time and share those services throughout the year. It was in the vet's interest to keep the animals healthy and reduce the number of calls from farmers, rather than to ensure that the farmer needed to call for service and pay regularly.

Most dairy farmers milk their cows with absolute regularity at a minimum of twice a day, with some high-producing herds milking up to four times a day to lessen the weight of large volumes of milk in the udder of the cow. This daily milking routine goes on for about 300 to 320 days per year that the cow stays in milk. Some small herds are milked once a day for about the last 20 days of the production cycle but this is not usual for large herds. If a cow is left unmilked just once she is likely to reduce milk-production almost immediately and the rest of the season may see her *dried off* (giving no milk) and still consuming feed for no production. However, once-a-day milking is now being practised more widely in New Zealand for profit and lifestyle reasons. This is effective because the fall in milk yield is at least partially offset by labour and cost savings from milking once per day. This compares to some intensive farm systems in the United States that milk three or more times per day due to higher milk yields per cow and lower marginal labour costs.

Farmers who are contracted to supply liquid milk for human consumption (as opposed to milk for processing into butter, cheese, and so on — see milk) often have to manage their herd so that the contracted number of cows are in milk the year round, or the required minimum milk output is maintained. This is done by mating cows outside their natural mating time so that the period when each cow in the herd is giving maximum production is in rotation throughout the year.

Northern hemisphere farmers who keep cows in barns almost all the year usually manage their herds to give continuous production of milk so that they get paid all year round. In the southern hemisphere the cooperative dairying systems allow for two months on no productivity because their systems are designed to take advantage of maximum grass and milk production in the spring and because the milk processing plants pay bonuses in the dry (winter) season to carry the farmers through the mid-winter break from milking. It also means that cows have a rest from milk production when they are most heavily pregnant. Some year-round milk farms are penalised financially for over-production at any time in the year by being unable to sell their overproduction at current prices.

Artificial insemination (AI) is common in all high-production herds.

## Industrial Processing

Dairy plants process the raw milk they receive from farmers so as to extend its marketable life. Two main types of processes are employed: heat treatment to ensure the safety of milk for human consumption and to lengthen its shelf-life, and dehydrating dairy products such as butter, hard cheese and milk powders so that they can be stored.

## Cream and Butter

Today, milk is separated by large machines in bulk into cream and skim milk. The cream is processed to produce various consumer products, depending on its thickness, its suitability for culinary uses and consumer demand, which differs from place to place and country to country.

Today, milk is separated by large machines in bulk into cream and skim milk. The cream is processed to produce various consumer products, depending on its thickness, its suitability for culinary uses and consumer demand, which differs from place to place and country to country.

Some cream is dried and powdered, some is condensed (by evaporation) mixed with varying amounts of sugar and canned. Most cream from New Zealand and Australian factories is made into butter. This is done by churning the cream until the fat globules coagulate and form a monolithic mass. This butter mass is washed and, sometimes, salted to improve keeping qualities. The residual buttermilk goes on to further processing. The butter is packaged (25 to 50 kg boxes) and chilled for storage and sale. At a later stage these packages are broken down into home-consumption sized packs. Butter sells for about US$3200 a tonne on the international market in 2007 (an unusual high).

## Skimmed Milk

The product left after the cream is removed is called skim, or skimmed, milk. Reacting skim milk with rennet or with an acid makes casein curds from the milk solids in skim milk, with whey as a residual. To make a consumable liquid a portion of cream is returned to the skim milk to make *low fat milk* (semi-skimmed) for human consumption. By varying the amount of cream returned, producers can make a variety of low-fat milks to suit their local market. Other products, such as calcium, vitamin D, and flavouring, are also added to appeal to consumers.

## Casein

Casein is the predominant phosphoprotein found in fresh milk. It has a very wide range of uses from being a filler for human foods, such as in ice cream, to the manufacture of products such as fabric, adhesives, and plastics. However, in the US these assorted non-food uses have led to concerns over the import of substandard (non-food-grade) powders from other countries, such as China, that are then used to artificially bolster domestic cheese yield without the casein additive undergoing FDA inspection.

## Cheese

Cheese is another product made from milk. Whole milk is reacted to form curds that can be compressed, processed and stored to form cheese. In countries where milk is legally allowed to be processed without pasteurisation a wide range of cheeses can be made using the bacteria naturally in the milk. In most other countries, the range of cheeses is smaller and the use of artificial cheese curing is greater. Whey is also the byproduct of this process.

Cheese has historically been an important way of 'storing' milk over the year, and carrying over its nutritional value between prosperous years and fallow ones. It is a food product that, with bread and beer, dates back to prehistory in Middle Eastern and European cultures, and like them is subject to innumerable variety and local specificity. Although nowhere near as big as the market for cow's milk cheese, a considerable amount of cheese is made commercially from other milks, especially goat and sheep (see Roquefort cheese for a notable example).

## Whey

In earlier times whey was considered to be a waste product and it was, mostly, fed to pigs as a convenient means of disposal. Beginning about 1950, and mostly since about 1980, lactose and many other products, mainly food additives, are made from both casein and cheese whey.

## Yogurt

Yoghurt (or yogurt) making is a process similar to cheese making, only the process is arrested before the curd becomes very hard.

## Milk Powders

Milk is also processed by various drying processes into powders. Whole milk, skim milk, buttermilk, and whey products are dried into a powder form and used for human and animal consumption. The main difference between production of powders for human or for animal consumption is in the protection of the process and the product from contamination. Some people drink milk reconstituted from powdered milk, because milk is about 88 per cent water and it is much cheaper to transport the dried product. Dried skim milk powder is worth about US$5300 a tonne (mid-2007 prices) on the international market.

Historically, the milking and the processing took place in the same place: on a dairy farm. Later, cream was separated from the milk by machine, on the farm, and the cream was transported to a factory for buttermaking. The skim milk was fed to pigs. This allowed for the high cost of transport (taking the smallest volume high-value product), primitive trucks and the poor quality of roads. Only farms close to factories could afford to take whole milk, which was essential for cheesemaking in industrial quantities, to them. The development of refrigeration and better road transport, in the late 1950s, has meant that most farmers milk their cows and only temporarily store the milk in large refrigerated bulk tanks, whence it is later transported by truck to central processing facilities.

## Milking Machines

Milking machines are used to harvest milk from cows when manual milking becomes inefficient or labour intensive. The milking unit is the portion of a milking machine for removing milk from an udder. It is made up of a claw, four teatcups, (Shells and rubber liners) long milk tube, long pulsation tube, and a pulsator. The claw is an assembly that connects the short pulse tubes and short milk tubes from the teatcups to the long pulse tube and long milk tube. (Cluster assembly) Claws are commonly made of stainless steel or plastic or both. Teatcups are composed of a rigid outer shell (stainless steel or plastic) that holds a soft inner liner or *inflation*. Transparent sections in the shell may allow viewing of liner collapse and milk flow. The annular space between the shell and liner is called the pulse chamber.

Milking machines work in a way that is different from hand milking or calf suckling. Continuous vacuum is applied inside the soft liner to massage milk from the teat by creating a pressure difference across the teat canal (or opening at the end of the teat). Vacuum also helps keep the machine attached to the cow. The vacuum applied to the teat causes congestion of teat tissues (accumulation of blood and other fluids). Atmospheric air is admitted into the pulsation chamber about once per second (the pulsation rate) to allow the liner to collapse around the end of teat and relieve congestion in the teat tissue. The ratio of the time that the liner is open (milking phase) and closed (rest phase) is called the pulsation ratio.

The four streams of milk from the teatcups are usually combined in the claw and transported to the milkline, or the collection bucket (usually sized to the output of one cow) in a single milk hose. Milk is then transported (manually in buckets) or with a combination of airflow and mechanical pump to a central storage vat or bulk tank. Milk is refrigerated on the farm in most countries either by passing through a heat-exchanger or in the bulk tank, or both.

The two rigid stainless steel teatcup shells applied to the front two quarters of the udder are visible. The top of the flexible liner is visible at the top of the shells as are the short milk tubes and short pulsation tubes extending from the bottom of the shells to the claw. The bottom of the claw is transparent to allow observation of milk flow. When milking is completed the vacuum to the milking unit is shut off and the teatcups are removed.

Milking machines keep the milk enclosed and safe from external contamination. The interior 'milk contact' surfaces of the machine are kept clean by a manual or automated washing procedures implemented after milking is completed. Milk contact surfaces must comply with regulations requiring food-grade materials (typically stainless steel and special plastics and rubber compounds) and are easily cleaned.

Most milking machines are powered by electricity but, in case of electrical failure, there can be an alternative means of motive power, often an internal combustion engine, for the vacuum and milk pumps. Milk cows cannot tolerate delays in scheduled milking without serious milk production reductions.

## Milking Shed Layouts

***Bail-style sheds:*** This type of milking facility was the first development, after open-paddock milking, for many farmers. The building was a long, narrow, *lean-to* shed that was open along one long side. The cows were held in a yard at the open side and when they were about to be milked they were positioned in one of the bails (stalls). Usually the cows were restrained in the bail with a breech chain and a rope to restrain the outer back leg. The cow could not move about excessively and the milker could expect not to be kicked or trampled while sitting on a (three-legged) stool and milking into a bucket. When each cow was finished she backed out into the yard again. The UK bail, developed largely by Rex Patterson, was a six standing mobile shed with steps that the cow mounted, so the herdsman didn't have to bend so low. The milking equipment was much as today, a vacuum from a pump, pulsators, a claw-piece with pipes leading to the four shells and liners that stimulate and suck the milk from the teat. The milk went into churns, via a cooler.

As herd sizes increased a door was set into the front of each bail so that when the milking was done for any cow the milker could, after undoing the leg-rope and with a remote link, open the door and allow her to exit to the pasture. The door was closed, the next cow walked into the bail and was secured. When milking machines were introduced bails were set in pairs so that a cow was being milked in one paired bail while the other could be prepared for milking. When one was finished the machine's cups are swapped to the other cow. This is the same as for *Swingover Milking Parlours* as described below except that the cups are loaded on the udder from the side. As herd numbers increased it was easier to double-up the cup-sets and milk both cows simultaneously than to increase the number of bails. About 50 cows an hour can be milked in a shed with 8 bales by one person. using the same teat cups for successive cows has the danger of transmitting infection, mastitis, from one cow to another. Some farmers have devised their own ways to disinfect the clusters between cows.

***Herringbone Milking Parlours:*** In herringbone milking sheds, or parlours, cows enter, in single file, and line up almost perpendicular to the central aisle of the milking parlour on both sides of a central pit in which the milker works (you can visualise a fishbone with the ribs representing the cows and the spine being the milker's working area; the cows face outward). After washing the udder and teats the cups of the milking machine are applied to the cows, from the rear of their hind legs, on both sides of the working area. Large herringbone sheds can milk up to 600 cows efficiently with two people.

***Swingover Milking Parlours:*** Swingover parlours are the same as herringbone parlours except they have only one set of milking cups to be shared between the two rows of cows, as one side is being milked the cows on the other side are moved out and replaced with unmilked ones. The advantage of this system is that it is less costly to equip, however it operates at slightly better than half-speed and one would not normally try to milk more than about 100 cows with one person.

***Rotary Milking sheds:*** Rotary milking sheds consist of a turntable with about 12 to 100 individual stalls for cows around the outer edge. A 'good' rotary will be operated with 24–32 (~48–50+) stalls by one (two) milkers. The turntable is turned by an electric-motor drive at a rate that one turn is the time for a cow to be milked completely. As an empty stall passes the entrance a cow steps on, facing the centre, and rotates with the turntable. The next cow moves into the next vacant stall and so on. The operator, or milker, cleans the teats, attaches the cups and does any other feeding or whatever husbanding operations that are necessary. Cows are milked as the platform rotates. The milker, or an automatic device, removes the milking machine cups and the cow backs out and leaves at an exit just before the entrance. The rotary system is capable of milking very large herds — over a thousand cows.

***Automatic Milking sheds:*** Automatic milking or 'robotic milking' sheds can be seen in Australia, New Zealand and many European countries. Current automatic milking sheds use the voluntary milking (VM) method. These allow the cows to voluntarily present themselves for milking at any time of the day or night, although repeat visits may be limited by the farmer through computer software. A robot arm is used to clean teats and apply milking equipment, while automated gates direct cow traffic, eliminating the need for the farmer to be present during the process. The entire process is computer controlled.

*Supplementary accessories in sheds:* Farmers soon realised that a milking shed was a good place to feed cows supplementary foods that overcame local dietary deficiencies or added to the cows' well-being and production. Each bail might have a box into which such feed is delivered as the cow arrives so that she is eating while being milked. A computer can read the eartag of each beast to ration the correct individual supplement. A close alternative is to use 'out-of-parlour-feeders', stalls that respond to a transponder around the cow's neck that is programmed to provide each cow with a supplementary feed, the quantity dependent on her production, stage in lactation, and the benefits of the main ration.

The holding yard at the entrance of the shed is important as a means of keeping cows moving into the shed. Most yards have a powered gate that ensures that the cows are kept close to the shed.

Water is a vital commodity on a dairy farm: cows drink about 20 gallons (80 litres) a day, sheds need water to cool and clean them. Pumps and reservoirs are common at milking facilities. Water can be warmed by heat transfer with milk.

In countries where cows are grazed outside year-round, there is little waste disposal to deal with. The most concentrated waste is at the milking shed, where the animal waste is liquefied (during the water-washing process) and allowed to flow by gravity, or pumped, into composting ponds with anaerobic bacteria to consume the solids. The processed water and nutrients are then pumped back onto the pasture as irrigation and fertilizer. Surplus animals are slaughtered for processed meat and other rendered products.

In the associated milk processing factories, most of the waste is washing water that is treated, usually by composting, and returned to waterways. This is much different from half a century ago, when the main products were butter, cheese and casein, and the rest of the milk had to be disposed of as waste (sometimes as animal feed).

In areas where cows are housed all year round, the waste problem is difficult because of the amount of feed that is bought in and the amount of bedding material that also has to be removed and composted. The size of the problem can be understood by standing downwind of the barns where such dairying goes on.

In many cases, modern farms have very large quantities of milk to be transported to a factory for processing. If anything goes wrong with the milking, transport or processing facilities it can be a major disaster trying to dispose of enormous quantities of milk. If a road tanker overturns on a road, the rescue crew is looking at accommodating the spill of 5 to 10 thousand gallons of milk (20 to 45 thousand litres) without allowing any into the waterways. A derailed rail tanker-train may involve 10 times that amount. Without refrigeration, milk is a fragile commodity, and it is very damaging to the environment in its raw state A widespread electrical power blackout is another disaster for the dairy industry, because both milking and processing facilities are affected.

In dairy-intensive areas, the simplest way of disposing of large quantities of milk has been to dig a large hole in the ground and allow the clay to filter the milk solids as it soaks away. This is not very satisfactory.

## Associated Diseases

Leptospirosis is one of the most common debilitating diseases of milkers, made somewhat worse since the introduction of herringbone sheds, because of unavoidable direct contact with bovine urine.

Cowpox is one of the helpful diseases; it is barely harmful to humans and tends to inoculate them against other poxes such as small pox.

Tuberculosis (TB) is able to be transmitted from cattle mainly via milk products that are unpasteurised. TB has been eradicated from many countries by testing for the disease and culling suspected animals.

Brucellosis is a bacterial disease transmitted to humans by dairy products and direct animal contact. Brucellosis has been eradicated from certain countries by testing for the disease and culling suspected animals Listeria is a bacterial disease associated with unpasteurised milk, and can affect some cheeses made in traditional ways. Careful observance of the traditional cheesemaking methods achieves reasonable protection for the consumer. Johne's Disease (pronounced 'yo-knees') is a contagious, chronic and sometimes fatal infection in ruminants caused by a bacterium named Mycobacterium avium subspecies paratuberculosis M. paratuberculosis). The bacteria are present in retail milk, and are believed by some researchers to be the primary cause of Crohn's disease in humans. This disease is not known to infect animals in Australia and New Zealand.

2

# Milk

Milk is an opaque white liquid produced by the mammary glands of mammals. It provides the primary source of nutrition for young mammals before they are able to digest other types of food. The early lactation milk is known as colostrum, and carries the mother's antibodies to the baby. It can reduce the risk of many diseases in the baby. The exact components of raw milk varies by species, but it contains significant amounts of saturated fat, protein and calcium as well as vitamin C. Cow's milk has a pH ranging from 6.4 to 6.8, making it slightly acidic.

There are two distinct types of milk consumption — a natural source of nutrition for all infant mammals, and a food product for humans of all ages derived from other animals.

**Nutrition for Infant Mammals**

In almost all mammals, milk is fed to infants through breastfeeding, either directly or by expressing the milk to be stored and consumed later. Some cultures, historically or currently, continue to use breast milk to feed their children until they are seven years old.

## Food Product for Humans

In many cultures of the world, especially the Western world, humans continue to consume milk beyond infancy, using the milk of other animals (especially cattle, goats and sheep) as a food product. For millennia, cow's milk has been processed into dairy products such as cream, butter, yogurt, kefir, ice cream, and especially the more durable and easily transportable product, cheese. Modern industrial processes produce casein, whey protein, lactose, condensed milk, powdered milk, and many other food-additive and industrial products.

Humans are an exception in the natural world for consuming milk past infancy, despite the fact that more than 75 per cent of adult humans show some degree (some as little as 5%) of lactose intolerance, a characteristic that is more prevalent among individuals of African or Asian descent. The sugar lactose is found only in milk, forsythia flowers, and a few tropical shrubs. The enzyme needed to digest lactose, lactase, reaches its highest levels in the small intestines after birth and then begins a slow decline unless milk is consumed regularly. On the other hand, those groups that do continue to tolerate milk often have exercised great creativity in using the milk of domesticated ungulates, not only of cattle, but also sheep, goats, yaks, water buffalo, horses, and camels. The largest producer and consumer of cattle and buffalo milk in the world is India.

The term *milk* is also used for whitish non-animal substitutes such as soy milk, rice milk, almond milk, and coconut milk. Even the regurgitated substance secreted by glands in the mucosa of their upper digestive tract which pigeons feed their young is called crop milk though it bears little resemblance to mammalian milk.

## Grade A *vs* Grade B Milk

In the United States, there are two grades of milk, with Grade A primarily used for direct sales and consumption in stores, and Grade B used for indirect consumption, such as in cheesemaking or other processing.

The differences between the two grades are defined in the Wisconsin administrative code for Agriculture, Trade, and Consumer Protection, chapter 60. Grade B generally refers to milk that is cooled in milk cans, which are immersed in a bath of cold flowing water, typically drawn up from an underground water well rather than using mechanical refrigeration.

Grade A farms are inspected every 6 months, while Grade B farms are inspected every 2 years {WI-ATCP 60.24.2}.

Both types of farms are required to have two cleaning vats in the milkhouse for washing and rinsing of equipment {WI-ATCP 60.07.2(g)}. A farm must also have an additional separate sink and faucet provided for handwashing {WI-ATCP 60.07.2(h)}, unless the bulk tank was installed before Jan 1, 1979 or the farm uses milk cans.

Grade A milk stored in a bulk tank is cooled to 45 degrees F within 2 hours of milking. Grade A milk in a may only rise to 50 F if milk from additional milking sessions are added to the tank (potentially requiring a plate cooler to reduce the temperature of a large volume influx quickly enough) and must be cooled back to 45° F within two hours. {WI-ATCP 60.2.4(b)}.

Grade B milk in milk cans is cooled to 50 degrees F within 2 hours of milking. Grade B farms can not mix milk into cans from previous milking. {WI-ATCP 60.2.4(c)}.

The somatic cell count (SSC) of Grade A or B cow or sheep milk may not exceed 750,000 cells per mL, and the SCC of Grade A or B goat milk may not exceed 1,000,000 cells per mL. {WI-ATCP 60.15.4}.

The bacterial plate or loop count of Grade A milk may not exceed 100,000 per mL, while Grade B milk may not exceed 300,000 per mL. {WI-ATCP 60.15.2}.

A bacterial plate count test is required at least once a month. {WI-ATCP 60.18.3} If the bacterial count exceeds 100,000 per mL for Grade A or 300,000 per mL for grade B in 3 out of 5 tests, the license to sell milk is suspended. The license will be immediately revoked if the bacterial count ever exceeds 750,000 per mL. {WI-ATCP 60.18.6}.

Animal milk is first known to have been used as human food during the Secondary Products Revolution, around 5000BC. It is assumed that when animals such as cattle were first domesticated, it was only for purposes of meat. Cow's milk was first used as human food in the Middle East. Goats and sheep are ruminants: mammals adapted to survive on a diet of dry grass, a food source otherwise useless to humans, and one that is easily stockpiled. The animals dairying proved to be a more efficient way of turning uncultivated grasslands into sustenance: the food value of an animal killed for meat can be matched by perhaps one year's worth of milk from the same animal, which will keep producing milk — in convenient daily portions — for years.

Milk byproducts found inside stone age pottery from Turkey indicate processed milk was consumed in 6500 BC some thousands of years before the ability for adult humans to digest unprocessed milk had evolved.

DNA evidence extracted from Neolithic skeletons indicates that a thousand years later in 5500 BC people in Northern Europe were like all other peoples of the time and were still lactose intolerant.

Earthenware vessels found in England from a thousand years after this in 4500 BC contain milk byproducts indicating milk was used in some form although perhaps not drunk directly.

Milk was first delivered in bottles on January 11, 1878. The day is now remembered as *Milk Day* and is celebrated annually. The town of Harvard, Illinois also celebrates milk in the summer with a festival known as 'Milk Days'. Theirs is a different tradition meant to celebrate dairy farmers in the 'Milk Capital of the World'.

In addition to cattle, the following livestock animals provide milk used by humans for dairy products:

- Camel
- Donkey
- Goat
- Horse
- Reindeer
- Sheep
- Water buffalo
- Yak

In Russia and Sweden, small moose dairies also exist.

According to the National Bison Association, American Bison (also called American buffalo) are not milked commercially. However, various sources report cows resulting from cross-breeding bison and domestic cattle are good milk producers, both during the European settlement of North America and during the development of commercial Beefalo in the 1970s and 1980s.

Human milk is not produced or distributed industrially or commercially; however, milk banks exist that allow for the collection of donated human milk and its redistribution to infants who may benefit from human milk for various reasons (premature neonates, babies with allergies or metabolic diseases, etc.).

All other female mammals do produce milk, but are rarely or never used to produce dairy products for human consumption.

In the Western world today, cow's milk is produced on an industrial scale, and is by far the most commonly consumed form of milk. Commercial dairy farming using automated milking equipment produces the vast majority of milk in developed countries. Dairy cattle such as the Holstein have been specially bred for increased milk production. 90 per cent of the dairy cows in the United States and 85 per cent in Great Britain are Holsteins. Other dairy cows in the United States include Ayrshire, Brown Swiss, Guernsey, Jersey, and Milking Shorthorn (Dairy Shorthorn). The largest producers of dairy products and milk today are India followed by the United States, Germany, and Pakistan.

Increasing affluence in developing countries, as well as increased promotion of milk and milk products, has led to a rise in milk consumption in developing countries in recent years. In turn, the opportunities presented by these growing markets have attracted investment by multinational dairy firms. Nevertheless, in many countries production remains on a small-scale and presents significant opportunities for diversification of income sources by small farmers. Local milk collection centers, where milk is collected and chilled prior to being transferred to urban dairies, are a good example of where farmers have been able to work on a cooperative basis, particularly in countries such as India.

Milk is an emulsion or colloid of butterfat globules within a water-based fluid. Each fat globule is surrounded by a membrane consisting of phospholipids and proteins; these emulsifiers keep the individual globules from joining together into noticeable grains of butterfat and also protect the globules from the fat-digesting activity of enzymes found in the fluid portion of the milk. In unhomogenized cow's milk, the fat globules average about four micrometers across. The fat-soluble vitamins A, D, E, and K are found within the milkfat portion of the milk.

The largest structures in the fluid portion of the milk are casein protein micelles: aggregates of several thousand protein molecules, bonded with the help of nanometer-scale particles of calcium phosphate. Each micelle is roughly spherical and about a tenth of a micrometer across. There are four different types of casein proteins, and collectively they make up around 80 per cent of the protein in milk, by weight. Most of the casein proteins are bound into the micelles. There are several competing theories regarding the precise structure of the micelles, but they share one important feature: the outermost layer consists of strands of one type of protein, k-Casein, reaching out from the body of the micelle into the surrounding fluid. These Kappa-casein molecules all have a negative electrical charge and therefore repel each other, keeping the micelles separated under normal conditions and in a stable colloidal suspension in the water-based surrounding fluid.

A simplified representation of a lactose molecule being broken down into glucose and galactose.

Both the fat globules and the smaller casein micelles, which are just large enough to deflect light, contribute to the opaque white colour of milk. The fat globules contain some yellow-orange carotene, enough in some breeds (such as Guernsey and Jersey cattle) to impart a golden or 'creamy' hue to a glass of milk. The riboflavin in the whey portion of milk has a greenish colour, which can sometimes be discerned in skim milk or whey products. Fat-free skim milk has only the casein micelles to scatter light, and they tend to scatter shorter-wavelength blue light more than they do red, giving skim milk a bluish tint.

Milk contains dozens of other types of proteins besides the caseins. They are more water-soluble than the caseins and do not form larger structures. Because these proteins remain suspended in the whey left behind when the caseins coagulate into curds, they are collectively known as *whey proteins*. Whey proteins make up around twenty per cent of the protein in milk, by weight. Lactoglobulin is the most common whey protein by a large margin.

The carbohydrate lactose gives milk its sweet taste and contributes about 40 per cent of whole cow's milk's calories. Lactose is a composite of two simple sugars, glucose and galactose. In nature, lactose is found only in milk and a small number of plants. Other components found in raw cow's milk are living white blood cells, Mammary-gland cells, various bacteria, and a large number of active enzymes.

In most Western countries, a centralized dairy facility processes milk and products obtained from milk (dairy products), such as cream, butter, and cheese. In the U.S., these dairies are usually local companies, while in the Southern Hemisphere facilities may be run by very large nation-wide or trans-national corporations (such as Fonterra).

## Pasteurization

Pasteurization is used to kill harmful microorganisms by heating the milk for a short time and then cooling it for storage and transportation. Pasteurized milk is still perishable and must be stored cold by both suppliers and consumers. Dairies print expiration dates on each container, after which stores will remove any unsold milk from their shelves.

A newer process, Ultra Pasteurization or ultra-high temperature treatment (UHT), heats the milk to a higher temperature for a shorter time. This extends its shelf life and allows the milk to be stored unrefrigerated because of the longer lasting sterilization effect.

## Microfiltration

Microfiltration is a process that partially replaces pasteurization and produces milk with fewer microorganisms and longer shelf life without a change in the taste of the milk. In this process, cream is separated from the whey and is pasteurized in the usual way, but the whey is forced through ceramic microfilters that trap 99.9 per cent of microorganisms in the milk (as compared to 95% killing of microorganisms in conventional pasteurization). The whey is then recombined with the pasteurized cream to reconstitute the original milk composition.

## Creaming and Homogenization

Upon standing for 12 to 24 hours, fresh milk has a tendency to separate into a high-fat cream layer on top of a larger, low-fat milk layer. The cream is often sold as a separate product with its own uses; today the separation of the cream from the milk is usually accomplished rapidly in centrifugal cream separators. The fat globules rise to the top of a container of milk because fat is less dense than water. The smaller the globules, the more other molecular-level forces prevent this from happening. In fact, the cream rises in cow's milk much more quickly than a simple model would predict: rather than isolated globules, the fat in the milk tends to form into clusters containing about a million globules, held together by a number of minor whey proteins. These clusters rise faster than individual globules can. The fat globules in milk from goats, sheep, and water buffalo do not form clusters so readily and are smaller to begin with; cream is very slow to separate from these milks.

Milk is often homogenized, a treatment which prevents a cream layer from separating out of the milk. The milk is pumped at high pressures through very narrow tubes, breaking up the fat globules through turbulence and cavitation. A greater number of smaller particles possess more total surface area than a smaller number of larger ones, and the original fat globule membranes cannot completely cover them. Casein micelles are attracted to the newly-exposed fat surfaces; nearly one-third of the micelles in the milk end up participating in this new membrane structure. The casein weighs down the globules and interferes with the clustering that accelerated separation. The exposed fat globules are briefly vulnerable to certain enzymes present in milk, which could break down the fats and produce rancid flavors. To prevent this, the enzymes are inactivated by pasteurizing the milk immediately before or during homogenization.

Homogenized milk tastes blander but feels creamier in the mouth than unhomogenized; it is whiter and more resistant to developing off flavors. Creamline, or cream-top, milk is unhomogenized; it may or may not have been pasteurized. Milk which has undergone high-pressure homogenization, sometimes labeled as 'ultra-homogenized', has a longer shelf life than milk which has undergone ordinary homogenization at lower pressures. Homogenized milk may be more digestible than unhomogenized milk.

Kurt A. Oster, M.D., who worked in the 1960s through the 1980s, suggested a link between homogenized milk and arterosclerosis, due to damage to plasmalogen as a result of the release of bovine xanthine oxidase (BXO) from the milk fat globular membrane (MFGM) during homogenization. However, Oster's hypothesis has been widely criticized and has not been generally accepted by the scientific community. No link has been found between arterosclerosis and milk consumption.

The composition of milk differs widely between species. Factors such as the type of protein; the proportion of protein, fat, and sugar; the levels of various vitamins and minerals; and the size of the butterfat globules and the strength of the curd are among those than can vary. For example:

- Human milk contains, on average, 1.1 per cent protein, 4.2 per cent fat, 7.0 per cent lactose (a sugar), and supplies 72 kcal of energy per 100 grams.
- Cow's milk contains, on average, 3.4 per cent protein, 3.6 per cent fat, and 4.6 per cent lactose, 0.7 per cent minerals and supplies 66 kcal of energy per 100 grams. See also Nutritional value further on.
- Donkey and horse milk have the lowest fat content, while the milk of seals and whales can contain more than 50 per cent fat. High fat content

is not unique to aquatic mammals, as guinea pig milk has an average fat content of 46 per cent.

Processed milk began containing differing amounts of fat during the 1950s. 1 cup (250 ml) of 2 per cent-fat milk contains 285 mg of calcium, which represents 22 per cent to 29 per cent of the daily recommended intake (DRI) of calcium for an adult. Depending on the age, milk contains 8 grams of protein, and a number of other nutrients (either naturally or through fortification) including:

- Biotin
- Pantothenic acid
- Iodine
- Potassium
- Magnesium
- Selenium
- Thiamine
- Vitamin A
- Vitamin B12
- Riboflavin
- Vitamins D
- Vitamin K

The amount of calcium from milk that is absorbed by the human body is disputed. Calcium from dairy products has a greater bioavailability than calcium from certain vegetables, such as spinach, that contain high levels of calcium-chelating agents, but a similar or lesser bioavailability than calcium from low-oxalate vegetables such as kale, broccoli, or other vegetables in the Brassica genus.

Studies show possible links between low-fat milk consumption and reduced risk of arterial hypertension, coronary heart disease, colourectal cancer and obesity. Overweight individuals who drink milk may benefit from decreased risk of insulin resistance and type 2 diabetes. One study has shown that for women desiring to have a child, those who consume full fat dairy products may actually slightly increase their fertility, while those consuming low fat dairy products may slightly reduce their fertility. Milk is a source of Conjugated linoleic acid.

## Lactose Intolerance

Lactose, the disaccharide sugar component of all milk must be cleaved in the small intestine by the enzyme lactase in order for its constituents (galactose and glucose) to be absorbed. The production of this enzyme declines significantly after weaning in all mammals. Consequently, many humans become unable to properly digest lactose as they mature. There is a great deal of variance, with some individuals reacting badly to even small amounts of lactose, some able to consume moderate quantities, and some able to consume large quantities of milk and other dairy products without problems. When an individual consumes milk without producing sufficient lactase, they may suffer diarrhea, intestinal gas, cramps and bloating, as the undigested lactose travels through the gastrointestinal tract and serves as nourishment for intestinal microflora who excrete gas, a process known as anaerobic respiration.

It is estimated that 30 to 50 million Americans are lactose intolerant, including 75 per cent of Native Americans and African-Americans, and 90 per cent of Asian Americans. Lactose intolerance is less common among those descended from northern Europeans.

Lactose intolerance is a natural process and there is no reliable way to prevent or reverse it. Lactase is readily available in pill form, and many individuals can use it to briefly increase their tolerance for dairy products.

## Controversy

Other studies suggest that milk consumption may increase the risk of suffering from certain health problems.

Cow's milk allergy (CMA) is as an immunologically mediated adverse reaction to one or more cow's milk proteins. Rarely is it severe enough to cause death. Milk contains casein, a substance that breaks down in the human stomach to produce casomorphin, an opioid peptide. In the early 1990s it was hypothesized that casomorphin can cause or aggravate autism, and casein-free diets are widely promoted. Studies supporting these claims have had significant flaws, and the data are inadequate to guide autism treatment recommendations. Studies described in the book The China Study note a correlation between casein intake and the promotion of cancer cell growth when exposed to carcinogens. However other studies have shown whey protein offers a protective effect against colon cancer.

A study demonstrated that men who drink a large amount of milk and consume dairy products were at a slightly increased risk of developing Parkinson's disease; the effect for women was smaller. The reason behind this is not fully understood, and it also remains unclear why there is less of a risk for women. Several sources suggest a correlation between high calcium intake (2000 mg per day, or twice the US recommended daily allowance, equivalent to six or more glasses of milk per day) and prostate cancer. A large study specifically implicates dairy, i.e., low-fat milk and other dairy to which vitamin A palmitate has been added. A review published by the World Cancer Research Fund and the American Institute for Cancer Research states that at least eleven human population studies have linked excessive dairy product consumption and prostate cancer, however randomized clinical trial data with appropriate controls only exists for calcium, not dairy produce, where there was no correlation. Medical studies have also shown a possible link between milk consumption and the exacerbation of diseases such as Crohn's disease, Hirschsprung's disease—mimicking symptoms in babies with existing cow's milk allergies ,and the aggravation of Behçet's disease.

Since November 1993, with FDA approval, Monsanto has been selling recombinant bovine somatotropin (rbST), also called rBGH, to dairy farmers. Cows produce bovine growth hormone naturally, but some producers administer an additional recombinant version of BGH which is produced through a genetically-engineered E. coli because it increases milk production. Bovine growth horome also stimulates liver production of insulin-like growth factor 1 (IGF1). If rbST-treated cows produced milk with higher levels of IGF1 this would be of medical concern, because IGF1 stimulates cancer growth in humans. Elevated levels of IGF1 in human blood has been linked to increased rates of breast, colon, and prostate cancer. Monsanto has stated that both of these compounds are harmless given the levels found in milk and the effects of pasteurization. However Monsanto's own tests, conducted in 1987, demonstrated that statistically significant growth stimulating effects were induced in organs of adult rats by feeding IGF-1 at low dose levels for only two weeks. "Drinking rBGH milk would thus be expected to significantly increase IGF-1 blood levels and consequently to increase risks of developing breast cancer and promoting its invasiveness."

The EU has recommended against Monsanto milk On June 9, 2006, the largest milk processor in the world and the two largest supermarkets in the United States — Dean Foods, Wal-Mart, and Kroger — announced that they are "on a nationwide search for rBGH-free milk." Milk from cows given rBST may be sold in the United States, and the FDA stated that no significant difference has been shown between milk derived from rBST-treated and that from non-rBST-treated cows. Milk that advertises that it comes from cows not treated with rBST is required to state this finding on its label.

Cows receiving rBGH supplements may more frequently contract an udder infection known as mastitis. Problems with mastitis have led to Canada, Australia, New

Zealand, and Japan banning milk from rBST treated cows. Mastitis, among other diseases, may be responsible for the fact that levels of white blood cells in milk vary naturally.

**Ethical Concerns**

Vegans and some other vegetarians do not consume milk for a variety of reasons. They may object to features of dairy farming including the necessity of killing almost all the male offspring of dairy cows (either by disposal soon after birth, for veal production, or for beef), the routine separation of mother and calf soon after birth, other perceived inhumane treatment of dairy cattle, and culling of cows after their productive lives.

**Varieties and Brands**

Milk products are sold in a number of varieties based on types/degrees of:

- age (e.g., cheddar);
- additives (e.g., vitamins);
- coagulation (e.g., cottage cheese);
- farming method (e.g., organic, grass-fed);
- fat content (e.g., half and half);
- fermentation (e.g., buttermilk);
- flavouring (e.g., chocolate);
- homogenization (e.g., raw milk);
- mammal (e.g., cow, goat, sheep);
- packaging (e.g., bottle);
- sterilization (e.g., pasteurization);
- water content (e.g., dry milk);

Demeter certified milk is produced with biodynamic agriculture methods and is similar in standards to organic milk and biological milk, with a few special farm procedures added that are biodynamic-specific.

## Additives and Flavouring

In areas where the cattle (and often the people) live indoors, commercially sold milk commonly has vitamin D added to it to make up for lack of exposure to UVB radiation.

Reduced fat milks often have added vitamin A palmitate to compensate for the loss of the vitamin during fat removal, in the United States this results in reduced fat milks having a higher vitamin A content than whole milk.

To aid digestion in those with lactose intolerance, milk is available in some areas with added bacterial cultures such as *Lactobacillus acidophilus* ('acidophilus milk') and bifidobacteria ('a/B milk'). Another milk with *Lactococcus lactis* bacteria cultures ('cultured buttermilk') is often used in cooking to replace the traditional use of naturally soured milk, which has become rare due to the ubiquity of pasteurization which kills the naturally occurring lactococcus bacteria.

Milk often has flavouring added to it for better taste or as a means of improving sales. Chocolate milk has been sold for many years and has been followed more recently by such other flavours as strawberry and banana.

In the UK, milk can be delivered daily by a milkman who travels his local milk round (route) using a milk float (often battery powered) during the early hours. Milk is delivered in 1 pint glass bottles with aluminium foil tops. Silver top denotes full cream unhomogenized; red top full cream homogenized; red/silver top semi-skimmed; blue/silver check top skimmed; and gold top channel island.

Empty bottles are rinsed before being left outside for the milkman to collect and take back to the dairy for washing and reuse. Currently many milkmen operate franchises as opposed to being employed by the dairy and payment is made at regular intervals, by leaving a cheque; by cash collection; or direct debit.

Although there was a steep decline in doorstep delivery sales throughout the 1990s, the service is still prominent, as dairies have diversified and the service is becoming more popular again. The doorstep delivery of milk is seen as part of the UK's heritage, and is used by people up and down the country.

**Australia and New Zealand**

In Australia and New Zealand, prior to 'metrification', milk was generally distributed in 1 pint (568ml) glass bottles. In Australia there was a government funded 'free milk for school children' programme, and milk was distributed at morning recess in 1/3 pint bottles. With the conversion to metric measures, the milk industry were concerned that the replacement of the pint bottles with 500ml bottles would result in a 13.6 per cent drop in milk consumption. Hence, all pint bottles were recalled and replaced by 600ml bottles. With time, due to the steadily increasing cost of collecting, transporting, storing and cleaning glass bottles, they were replaced by cardboard cartons. A number of designs were used, including a tetrahedron which could be close-packed without waste space, and could not be knocked over accidentally. (*slogan*: 'No more crying over spilt milk'.) However, the industry eventually settled on a design similar to that used in the United States.

However, the industry eventually settled on a design similar to that used in the United States. Milk is now availability in a variety of sizes in cardboard cartons (250ml, 375ml, 600ml, 1 litre and 1.5 litres) and plastic bottles (1 in NZ , 1.1 in Australia, 2 and 3 litres). A significant addition to the marketplace has been 'long life' milk (UHT), generally available in 1 and 2 litre rectangular cardboard cartons. In urban and suburban areas where there is sufficient demand, home delivery is still available, though in suburban areas this is often 3 times per week rather than daily. Another significant and popular addition to the marketplace has been flavoured milks — for example, as mentioned above, Farmers Union Iced Coffee outsells Coca-Cola in South Australia.

## India

In rural India milk is delivered daily by a local milkman carrying bulk quantities in a metal container, usually on a bicycle; and in other parts of metropolitan India, milk is usually bought or delivered in a plastic bags or cartons via shops or supermarkets.

## United States

In the United States, glass milk bottles have been mostly replaced with milk cartons (tall paper boxes with a square cross-section and a peaked top that can be folded outward upon opening to form a spout) and plastic jugs. Gallons of milk are almost always sold in jugs, while half-gallons and quarts may be found in both paper cartons and plastic jugs, and smaller sizes are almost always in cartons. Recently, milk has been sold in smaller resealable bottles made to fit in automobile cup holders. These individual serving sizes are also sold in flavored varieties.

The half-pint milk carton is the traditional unit as a component of school lunches.

## UHT Milk

Milk preserved by the UHT process is sold in cartons often called a brick that lack the peak of the traditional milk carton. Milk preserved in this fashion does not need to be refrigerated before opening and has a longer shelf life than milk in ordinary packaging. It is more typically sold unrefrigerated on the shelves in Europe and Latin America than in the United States. In Australia it is generally sold unrefrigerated, though some supermarkets also keep small quantities refrigerated.

## Glass

Glass milk containers are now rare. Most people purchase milk in bags, plastic bottles, or plastic-coated paper cartons. Ultraviolet (UV) light from fluorescent lighting can alter the flavor of milk, so many companies that once distributed milk in transparent or highly translucent containers are now using thicker materials that block the UV light. Many people feel that such 'UV protected' milk tastes better.

## Packaging

Milk comes in a variety of containers with local variants.

### Australia and New Zealand

Distributed in a variety of sizes, most commonly in aseptic cartons for up to 1.5 litres, and plastic screw-top bottles beyond that with the following volumes; 1.1L, 2L, and 3L. 1 litre milk bags are starting to appear in supermarkets, but have not yet proved popular. Most UHT-milk is packed in 1 or 2 litre paper containers with a sealed plastic spout.

Used to be sold in cooled 1 litre bags, just like in South Africa. Nowadays the most common form is 1 litre aseptic cartons containing UHT skimmed, semi-skimmed or whole milk, although the plastic bags are still in use for pasteurized milk. Higher grades of pasteurized milk can be found in cartons or plastic bottles. Sizes other than 1 liter are rare.

### Canada

1.33 litre plastic bags (sold as 4 litres in 3 bags) are widely available in some areas (especially the Maritimes, Ontario and Quebec), although the 4 litre plastic jug has supplanted them in western Canada. Other common packaging sizes are 2 litre, 1 litre, 500 millilitre, and 250 millilitre cartons, as well as 4 litre, 1 litre, 250 ml aseptic cartons and 500 ml plastic jugs.

### China

Sweetened milk is a drink popular with students of all ages and is often sold in small plastic bags complete with straw. Adults not wishing to drink at a banquet often drink milk served from cartons or milk tea.

**Parts of Europe**

Sizes of 500 millilitres, 1 litre (the most common), 1.5 litres, 2 litres and 3 litres are commonplace.

**Finland**

Commonly sold in 1l or 1.5l cartons, in some places also in 2dl and 5dl cartons.

**Hong Kong**

Milk is sold in glass bottles (220 ml), cartons (236 ml and 1L), plastic jugs (2 litres) and aseptic cartons (250 ml).

**Israel**

Non-UHT milk is most commonly sold in 1 litre waxed cardboard boxes and 1 litre plastic bags. It may also be found in 0.5L and 2L waxed cardboard boxes, 2L plastic jugs and 1L plastic bottles. UHT milk is available in 1 litre (and less commonly also in 0.25L) carton "bricks".

**Japan**

Commonly sold in 1 litre waxed paperboard cartons. In most city centers there is also home delivery of milk in glass jugs. As seen in China, sweetened and flavoured milk drinks are commonly seen in vending machines.

**South Africa**

Commonly sold in 1 litre bags. The bag is then placed in a plastic jug and the corner cut off before the milk is poured.

**South Korea**

Sold in cartons (180ml, 200ml, 500ml 900ml, 1L, 1.8L, 2.3L), plastic jugs (1L and 1.8L), aseptic cartons (180ml and 200ml) and plastic bags (1L).

**Sweden**

Commonly sold in 0.3L, 1L or 1.5L cartons and sometimes as plastic or glass milk bottles.

**Poland**

UHT milk is mostly sold in aseptic cartons (500ml, 1L, 2L), and non-UHT in 1L plastic bags or plastic bottles. Milk, UHT is commonly boiled, despite being pasteurized.

When raw milk is left standing for a while, it turns 'sour'. This is the result of fermentation, where lactic acid bacteria ferment the lactose inside the milk into lactic acid. Prolonged fermentation may render the milk unpleasant to consume. This fermentation process is exploited by the introduction of bacterial cultures (e.g. *Lactobacilli sp., Streptococcus sp., Leuconostoc sp.*, etc) to produce a variety of fermented milk products. The reduced pH from lactic acid accumulation denatures proteins and caused the milk to undergo a variety of different transformations in appearance and texture, ranging from an aggregate to smooth consistency. Some of these products include sour cream, yoghurt, cheese, buttermilk, viili, kefir and kumis. *See Dairy product* for more information.

Pasteurization of cow's milk initially destroys any potential pathogens and increases the shelf-life , but eventually results in spoilage that makes it unsuitable for consumption. This causes it to assume an unpleasant odor, and the milk is deemed non-consumable due to unpleasant taste and an increased risk of food poisoning. In raw milk, the presence of lactic acid-producing bacteria, under suitable conditions, ferments the lactose present to lactic acid. The increasing acidity in turn prevents the growth of other organisms, or slows their growth significantly. During pasteurization however, these lactic acid bacteria are mostly destroyed.

In order to prevent spoilage, milk can be kept refrigerated and stored between 1 and 4 degrees Celsius in bulk tanks. Most milk is pasteurized by heating briefly and then refrigerated to allow transport from factory farms to local markets. The spoilage of milk can be forestalled by using ultra-high temperature (UHT) treatment; milk so treated can be stored unrefrigerated for several months until opened. Condensed milk, made by removing most of the water, can be stored in cans for many years, unrefrigerated, as can evaporated milk. The most durable form of milk is milk powder, which is produced from milk by removing almost all water. The moisture content is usually less than five per cent in both drum and spray dried milk powder.

**Language and Culture**

The importance of milk in human culture is attested to by the numerous expressions embedded in our languages, for example 'the milk of human kindness'. In ancient Greek mythology, the goddess Hera spilled her breast milk after refusing to feed Heracles, resulting in the Milky Way.

In African and Asian developing nations, butter is traditionally made from fermented milk rather than cream. It can take several hours of churning to produce workable butter grains from fermented milk.

Holy books have also mentioned milk; the Bible contains references to the 'Land of Milk and Honey'. In the Quran, there is a request to wonder on milk as follows: 'And surely in the livestock there is a lesson for you, We give you to drink of that which is in their bellies from the midst of digested food and blood, pure milk palatable for the drinkers.'(16-The Honeybee, 66). The Ramadhan fast is traditionally broken with a glass of milk and dates.

The verb, 'to milk' something is often used in the vernacular of many English-speaking countries as a synonym for extortion or, in less loaded terms, taking advantage of a situation where one has another person at a disadvantage, as in 'milking the situation'.

The word milk has had many slang meanings over time. In the early 17th century the word was used to mean semen, or vaginal secretions, or to masturbate oneself or someone else. In the 19th century, milk was used to describe a cheap alcoholic drink made from methylated spirits mixed with water. The word was also used to mean defraud, to be idle, to intercept telegrams addressed to someone else, and a weakling or 'milksop'. In the mid 1930s, the word was used in Australia meaning to siphon gas from a car.

Milk is sometimes referred to as moo juice in American English, while Cockney rhyming slang calls it Acker Bilk, Tom Silk, Lady in Silk and Kilroy Silk.

3

# Dairy Farming

Dairy farming is a class of agricultural, or an animal husbandry, enterprise, for long-term production of milk, usually from dairy cows but also from goats and sheep, which may be either processed on-site or transported to a dairy factory for processing and eventual retail sale.

Most dairy farms sell the male calves born by their cows, usually for veal production, or breeding depending on quality of the bull calf, rather than raising non-milk-producing stock. Many dairy farms also grow their own feed, typically including corn, alfalfa, and hay. This is fed directly to the cows, or is stored as silage for use during the winter season. Additional dietary supplements are often added to the feed to increase quality milk production.

Dairy farming has been part of agriculture for thousands of years. Historically it has been one part of small, diverse farms. In the last century or so larger farms doing only dairy production have emerged. Large scale dairy farming is only viable where either a large amount of milk is required for production of more durable dairy products such as cheese, or there is a substantial market of people with cash to buy milk, but no cows of their own.

## Hand Milking

Centralized dairy farming as we understand it primarily developed around villages and cities, where residents were unable to have cows of their own due to a lack of grazing land. Near the town, farmers could make some extra money on the side by having additional animals and selling the milk in town. The dairy farmers would fill barrels with milk in the morning and bring it to market on a wagon. Until the late 1800s, the milking of the cow was done by hand. In the United States, several large dairy operations existed in some northeastern states and in the west, that involved as many as several hundred cows, but an individual milker could not be expected to milk more than a dozen cows a day. Smaller operations predominated.

Milking took place indoors in a barn with the cattle tied by the neck with ropes or held in place by stanchions. Feeding could occur simultaneously with milking in the barn, although most dairy cattle were pastured during the day between milkings. Such examples of this method of dairy farming are difficult to locate, but some are preserved as a historic site for a glimpse into the days gone by. One such instance that is open for this is at Point Reyes National Seashore.

## Vacuum Bucket Milking

The first milking machines were an extension of the traditional milking pail. The early milker device fit on top of a regular milk pail and sat on the floor under the cow. Following each cow being milked, the bucket would be dumped into a holding tank. This developed into the Surge hanging milker. Prior to milking a cow, a large wide leather strap called a surcingle was put around the cow, across the cow's lower back. The milker device and collection tank hung underneath the cow from the strap. This innovation allowed the cow to move around naturally during the milking process rather than having to stand perfectly still over a bucket on the floor.

With the availability of electric power and suction milking machines, the production levels that were possible in stanchion barns increased but the scale of the operations continued to be limited by the labor intensive nature of the milking process. Attaching and removing milking machines involved repeated heavy lifting of the machinery and its contents several times per cow and the pouring of the milk into milk cans. As a result, it was rare to find single-farmer operations of more than 50 head of cattle.

### Step-saver Milk Transport

As herd size began to increase, the bucket milker system became laborious. A vacuum milk-transport system known as the Step-Saver was developed to transport milk to the storage tank. The system used a long vacuum hose coiled around a receiver cart, and connected to a vacuum-breaker device in the milkhouse, allowing farmers to milk many cows without the necessity of walking increasingly longer distances carrying heavy buckets of milk.

### Milking Pipeline

The next innovation in automatic milking was the milk pipeline. This uses a permanent milk-return pipe and a second vacuum pipe that encircles the barn or milking parlour above the rows of cows, with quick-seal entry ports above each cow. By eliminating the need for the milk container, the milking device shrank in size and weight to the point where it could hang under the cow, held up only by the sucking force of the milker nipples on the cow's udder. The milk is pulled up into the milk-return pipe by the vacuum system, and then flows by gravity to the milkhouse vacuum-breaker that puts the milk in the storage tank.

The pipeline system greatly reduced the physical labor of milking since the farmer no longer needed to carry around huge heavy buckets of milk from each cow.

The pipeline allowed barn length to keep increasing and expanding, but after a point farmers started to milk the cows in large groups, filling the barn with one-half to one-third of the herd, milking the animals, and then emptying and refilling the barn. As herd sizes continued to increase, this evolved into the more efficient milking parlour.

## Milking Parlours

Innovation in milking focussed on mechanising the milking parlour to maximise throughput of cows per operator which streamlined the milking process to permit cows to be milked as if on an assembly line, and to reduce physical stresses on the farmer by putting the cows on a platform slightly above the person milking the cows to eliminate having to constantly bend over. Many older and smaller farms still have tie-stall or stanchion barns, but worldwide a majority of commercial farms have parlours.

The milking parlour allowed a concentration of money into a small area, so that more technical monitoring and measuring equipment could be devoted to each milking station in the parlour. Rather than simply milking into a common pipeline for example, the parlour can be equipped with fixed measurement systems that monitor milk volume and record milking statistics for each animal. Tags on the animals allow the parlour system to automatically identify each animal as it enters the parlour.

## Recessed Parlours

More modern farms use recessed parlours, where the milker stands in a recess such that his arms are at the level of the cow's udder. Recessed parlors can be herringbone, where the cows stand in two angled rows either side of the recess and the milker accesses the udder from the side, parallel, where the cows stand side-by-side and the milker accesses the udder from the rear or, more recently, rotary (or carousel), where the cows are on a raised circular platform, facing the center of the circle, and the platform rotates while the milker stands in one place and accesses the udder from the rear. There are many other styles of milking parlours which are less common.

## Herringbone and Parallel Parlours

In herringbone and parallel parlours, the milker generally milks one row at a time. The milker will move a row of cows from the holding yard into the milking parlor, and milk each cow in that row. Once all or most of the milking machines have been removed from the milked row, the milker releases the cows to their feed. A new group of cows is then loaded into the now vacant side and the process repeats until all cows are milked.

## Rotary Parlours

In rotary parlours, the cows are loaded one at a time onto the platform as it slowly rotates. The milker stands near the entry to the parlor and puts the cups on the cows as they move past. By the time the platform has completed almost a full rotation, another milker or a machine removes the cups and the cow steps backwards off the platform and then walks to its feed.

## Automatic Milker Take-off

It can be harmful to an animal for it to be over-milked past the point where the udder has stopped releasing milk. Consequently the milking process involves not just applying the milker, but also monitoring the process to determine when the animal has been *milked out* and the milker should be removed. While parlor operations allowed a farmer to milk many more animals much more quickly, it also increased the number of animals to be monitored simultaneously by the farmer. The automatic take-off system was developed to remove the milker from the cow when the milk flow reaches a preset level, relieving the farmer of the duties of carefully watching over 20 or more animals being milked at the same time.

## Fully Automated Robotic Milking

In the 1980s and 1990s, robotic milking systems were developed and introduced (principally in the EU). Thousands of these systems are now in routine operation. In these systems the cow has a high degree of autonomy to choose her time of milking within pre-defined windows. These systems are generally limited to intensively managed systems although research continues to match them to the requirements of grazing cattle and to develop sensors to detect animal health and fertility automatically.

## History of Milk Preservation Methods

Cool temperature has been the main method by which milk freshness has been extended. When windmills and well pumps were invented, one of its first uses on the farm besides providing water for animals was for cooling milk, to extend the storage life before being transported to the town market.

The naturally cold underground water would be continuously pumped into a tub or other containers of milk set in the tub to cool after milking. This method of milk cooling was extremely popular before the arrival of electricity and refrigeration.

## Refrigeration

When refrigeration first arrived (the 19th century) the equipment was initially used to cool cans of milk, which were filled by hand milking. These cans were placed into a cooled water bath to remove heat and keep them cool until they were able to be transported to a collection facility. As more automated methods were developed for harvesting milk, hand milking was replaced and, as a result, the milk can was replaced by a bulk milk cooler. 'Ice banks' were the first type of bulk milk cooler. This was a double wall vessel with evaporator coils and water located between the walls at the bottom and sides of the tank. A small refrigeration compressor was used to remove heat from the evaporator coils. Ice eventually builds up around the coils, until it reaches a thickness of about three inches surrounding each pipe, and the cooling system shuts off. When the milking operation starts, only the milk agitator and the water circulation pump, which flows water across the ice and the steel walls of the tank, are needed to reduce the incoming milk to a temperature below 40 degrees.

This cooling method worked well for smaller dairies, however was fairly inefficient and was unable to meet the increasingly higher cooling demand of larger milking parlors. In the mid 1950's direct expansion refrigeration was first applied directly to the bulk milk cooler. This type of cooling utilizes an evaporator built directly into the inner wall of the storage tank to remove heat from the milk. Direct expansion is able to cool milk at a much faster rate than early ice bank type coolers and is still the primary method for bulk tank cooling today on small to medium sized operations.

Another device which has contributed significantly to milk quality is the plate heat exchanger (PHE). This device utilizes a number of specially designed stainless steel plates with small spaces between them. Milk is passed between every other set of plates with water being passed between the balance of the plates to remove heat from the milk. This method of cooling can remove large amounts of heat from the milk in a very short time, thus drastically slowing bacteria growth and thereby improving milk quality. Ground water is the most common source of cooling medium for this device. Dairy cows consume approximately 3 gallons of water for every gallon of milk production and prefer to drink slightly warm water as opposed to cold ground water. For this reason, PHE's can result in drastically improved milk quality, reduced operating costs for the dairymen by reducing the refrigeration load on his bulk milk cooler, and increased milk production by supplying the cows with a source of fresh warm water.

Plate heat exchangers have also evolved as a result of the increase of dairy farm herd sizes in the US. As a dairyman increases the size of his herd, he must also increase the capacity of his milking parlor in order to harvest the additional milk. This increase in parlor sizes has resulted in tremendous increases in milk throughput and cooling demand. Today's larger farms produce milk at a rate which direct expansion refrigeration systems on bulk milk coolers cannot cool in a timely manner.

PHE's are typically utilized in this instance to rapidly cool the milk to the desired temperature (or close to it) before it reaches the bulk milk tank. Typically, ground water is still utilized to provide some initial cooling to bring the milk to between 55 and 70 degrees F.A second (and sometimes third) section of the PHE is added to remove the remaining heat with a mixture of chilled pure water and propylene glycol. These chiller systems can be made to incorporate large evaporator surface areas and high chilled water flow rates to cool high flow rates of milk.

## Milking Operation

Milking machines are held in place automatically by a vacuum system that draws the ambient air pressure down from 15 to 21 pounds of vacuum. The vacuum is also used to lift milk vertically through small diameter hoses, into the receiving can. A milk lift pump draws the milk from the receiving can through large diameter stainless steel piping, through the plate cooler, then into a refrigerated bulk tank.

Milk is extracted from the cow's udder by flexible rubber sheaths known as liners or inflations that are surrounded by a rigid air chamber. A pulsating flow of ambient air and vacuum is applied to the inflation's air chamber during the milking process. When ambient air is allowed to enter the chamber, the vacuum inside the inflation causes the inflation to collapse around the cow's teat, squeezing the milk out of teat in a similar fashion as a baby calf's mouth massaging the teat. When the vacuum is reapplied in the chamber the flexible rubber inflation relaxes and opens up, preparing for the next squeezing cycle.

It takes the average cow three to five minutes to give her milk. Some cows are faster or slower. Slow-milking cows may take up to fifteen minutes to let down all their milk. Milking speed is only minorly related to the quantity of milk the cow produces – milking speed is a separate factor from milk quantity; milk quantity is not determinative of milking speed. Because most milkers milk cattle in groups, the milker can only process a group of cows at the speed of the slowest-milking cow. For this reason, many farmers will cull slow-milking cows.

The extracted milk passes through a strainer and plate heat exchangers before entering the tank, where it can be stored safely for a few days at approximately 3 °C or around 42 °F (6 °C). At pre-arranged times, a milk truck arrives and pumps the milk from the tank for transport to a dairy factory where it will be pasteurized and processed into many products.

## Animal Waste from Large Dairies

As measured in phosphorus, the waste output of 5,000 cows roughly equals a municipality of 70,000 people. In the U.S., dairy operations with more than 1,000 cows meet the EPA definition of a CAFO (Concentrated Animal Feeding Operation), and are subject to EPA regulations. For example, in the San Joaquin Valley of California a number of dairies have been established on a very large scale. Each dairy consists of several modern milking parlor set-ups operated as a single enterprise. Each milking parlor is surrounded by a set of 3 or 4 loafing barns housing 1,500 or 2,000 cattle. Some of the larger dairies have planned 10 or more series of loafing barns and milking parlours in this arrangement, so that the total operation may include as many as 15,000 or 20,000 cows. The milking process for these dairies is similar to a smaller dairy with a single milking parlour but repeated several times. The size and concentration of cattle creates major environmental issues associated with manure handling and disposal, which requires substantial areas of cropland (a ratio of 5 or 6 cows to the acre, or several thousand acres for dairies of this size) for manure spreading and dispersion, or several-acre methane digesters. Air pollution from methane gas associated with manure management also is a major concern. As a result, proposals to develop dairies of this size can be controversial and provoke substantial opposition from environmentalists including the Sierra Club and local activists.

The potential impact of large dairies was demonstrated when a massive manure spill occurred on a 5,000-cow dairy in Upstate New York, contaminating a 20-mile (32 km) stretch of the Black River, and killing 375,000 fish. On Aug. 10, 2005, a manure storage lagoon collapsed releasing several million gallons of manure into the Black River. Subsequently the New York Department of Environmental Conservation mandated a settlement package of $2.2 million against the dairy.

It is possible to maintain higher milk production by injecting cows with growth hormones known as recombinant BST or rBGH, but this is controversial due to its effects on animal and possibly human health. The European Union, Japan, Australia, New Zealand and Canada have banned its use due to these concerns. However, no such prohibition exists in the US, where approximately 17.2 per cent of dairy cows are treated in this way. The U.S. Food and Drug Administration states that no 'significant difference' has been found between milk from treated and non-treated cows but based on consumer concerns several milk purchasers and resellers have elected not to purchase milk produced with rBST.

## Management of the Herd

Modern dairy farmers use milking machines and sophisticated plumbing systems to harvest and store the milk from the cows, which are usually milked two or three times daily. During the warm months, in the northern hemisphere, cows may be allowed to graze in their pastures, both day and night, and are brought into the barn only to be milked. Many barns also incorporate tunnel ventilation into the architecture of the barn structure. This ventilation system is highly efficient and involves opening both ends of the structure allowing cool air to blow through the building. Farmers with this type of structure keep cows inside during the summer months to prevent sunburn and damage to udders. During the winter months, especially in northern climates, the cows may spend the majority of their time inside the barn, which is warmed by their collective body heat. Even in winter, the heat produced by the cattle requires the barns to be ventilated for cooling purposes. Many modern facilities, and particularly those in tropical areas, keep all animals inside at all times to facilitate herd management. Housing the cow can be either loose housed or stalls (called cow cubicles in UK). There is little research available on dimensions required for cow stalls, and much housing can be out of date, however increasingly companies are making farmers aware of the benefits, in terms of animal welfare, health and milk production.

In the southern hemisphere cows spend most of their lives outside on pasture, although they may receive supplementation during periods of low pasture availabliity.

The production of milk requires that the cow be in lactation, which is a result of the cow having given birth to a calf. The cycle of insemination, pregnancy, parturition, and lactation, followed by a 'dry' period of a few weeks before calving which allows udder tissue to regenerate. Dairy operations therefore include both the production of milk and the production of calves. Bull calves are either castrated and raised as steers for beef production or veal.

## Health and Well-being

Common ailments affecting dairy cows include infectious disease (e.g. mastitis, endometritis and digital dermatitis), metabolic disease (e.g. milk fever and ketosis) and injuries caused by their environment (e.g. hoof and hock lesions).

Lameness is commonly considered one of the most significant animal welfare issues for dairy cattle. It can be caused by a number of sources, including infections of the hoof tissue (e.g. fungal infections that cause dermatitis) and physical damage causing bruising or lesions (e.g. ulcers or hemorrhage of the hoof). While housing and management features common in modern conventional dairy farms (such as concrete barn floors, limited access to pasture and suboptimal bed-stall design) have been identified as contributing risk factors , small farms in developing countries can also demonstrate high rates.

India is the largest producer of dairy products in the world. There is a great deal of variation in the pattern of dairy production worldwide. Many countries which are large producers, consume this internally, while others — in particular New Zealand — export a large percentage of their production. Internal consumption is often in the form of liquid milk, while the bulk of international trade is in processed dairy products such as milk powder.

The world's largest exporter of dairy products is New Zealand, and dairy products are the largest export earner for the country. Fonterra is the fifth-largest dairy company in the world and New Zealand's largest company by turnover, Japan is the world's largest importer of dairy products.

**European Union**

The European Union is the largest milk producer in the world, with 143.7 million tonnes in 2003. This data, encompassing the present 25 member countries, can be further broken down into the production of the original 15 member countries, with 122 million tonnes, and the new 10 mainly former Eastern European countries with 21.7 million tonnes.

Dairy production is heavily distorted due to the Common Agricultural Policy — being subsidized in some areas, and subject to production quotas in other.

In the United States, the top four dairy states are, in order by total milk production; California, Wisconsin, New York, and Idaho. Dairy farming is also an important industry in Florida, Minnesota, Ohio and Vermont. There are 65,000 dairy farms in the United States.

Pennsylvania however, is the state with the heaviest dependence on dairy farming – there it is the number one industry. Pennsylvania is home to 8,500 farms and 555,000 dairy cows. Milk produced in Pennsylvania yields about US$1.5 billion in farm revenue every year, and is sold to various states up and down the east coast.

Milk prices collapsed in 2009. Senator Bernie Sanders accused Dean Foods of controlling 40 per cent of the country's milk market. He has requested the United States Department of Justice to pursue 'an anti-trust investigation. Dean Foods says it buys 15 per cent of the country's raw milk.

## Competition

Most milk-consuming countries have a local dairy farming industry, and most producing countries maintain significant subsidies and trade barriers to protect domestic producers from foreign competition. In large countries, dairy farming tends to be geographically clustered in regions with abundant natural water supplies (both for feed crops and for cattle) and relatively inexpensive land (even under the most generous subsidy regimes, dairy farms have poor return on capital). New Zealand, the fourth largest dairy producing country, does not apply any subsidies to dairy production.

The milking of cows was traditionally a labour-intensive operation and still is in less developed countries. Small farms need several people to milk and care for only a few dozen cows, though for many farms these employees have traditionally been the children of the farm family, giving rise to the term 'family farm'.

Advances in technology have mostly led to the radical redefinition of 'family farms' in industrialized countries such as the United States. With farms of hundreds of cows producing large volumes of milk, the larger and more efficient dairy farms are more able to weather severe changes in milk price and operate profitably, while 'traditional' very small farms generally do not have the equity or cash flow to do so. The common public perception of large corporate farms supplanting smaller ones is generally a misconception, as many small family farms expand to take advantage of economies of scale, and incorporate the business to limit the legal liabilities of the owners and simplify such things as tax management.

Before large scale mechanization arrived in the 1950s, keeping a dozen milk cows for the sale of milk was profitable. Now most dairies must have more than one hundred cows being milked at a time in order to be profitable, with other cows and heifers waiting to be "freshened" to join the milking herd . In New Zealand the average herd size, depending on the region, is about 350 cows.

Herd size in the US varies between 1,200 on the West Coast and Southwest, where large farms are commonplace, to roughly 50 in the Northeast, where land-base is a significant limiting factor to herd size. The average herd size in the U.S. is about one hundred cows per farm.

Currently, concerns regarding monopolies created by Dean Foods, Kraft, and other major buyers of bulk dairy products on the Chicago Mercantile Exchange have been raised, as American dairy farms have suffered extreme price depression and chaotic fluctuations while processors and retailers report record profits. Many theorize that unregulated imports of milk protein concentrate used by processors to boost cheese yield has artificially and unfairly influenced the markets in an effort to force consolidation and vertical integration in what has historically been a highly diversified industry.

4

# Pasteurization

Pasteurization is a process which slows microbial growth in food. The process was named after its creator, French chemist and microbiologist Louis Pasteur. The first pasteurization test was completed by Louis Pasteur and Claude Bernard on April 20, 1864. The process was originally conceived as a way of preventing wine and beer from souring.

Pasteurization is not intended to destroy all pathogenic micro-organisms in the food or liquid. Instead, pasteurization aims to reduce the number of viable pathogens so they are unlikely to cause disease (assuming pasteurization product is stored as indicated and consumed before its expiration date). Commercial-scale sterilisation of food is not common because it adversely affects the taste and quality of the product. Certain food products are processed to achieve the state of commercial sterility.

A newer method called flash pasteurization involves shorter exposure to higher temperatures, and is claimed to be better for preserving fashion and taste in some eggs.

The term cold pasteurization is used sometimes for the use of ionizing radiation (see Food irradiation) or other means (e.g. chemical) to kill bacteria in food. Food irradiation is also sometimes called pasteurization.

Another means of pasteurization is using pressure called high pressure pasteurization (HPP) also known as High pressure food preservation where extremely high pressure is used to kill the bacteria.

Steam pasteurization is used for continuous feed applications. This process significantly reduces the initial microbe count without irradiation, chemicals, or other potentially unsafe alternative treatments. Pasteurization means heating water up to 80 degrees Celsius.

Pasteurization is typically associated with milk, first suggested by Franz von Soxhlet in 1886. High Temperature Short Time (HTST) pasteurised milk typically has a refrigerated shelf life of two to three weeks, whereas ultra pasteurised milk can last much longer when refrigerated, sometimes two to three months. When UHT treatment is combined with sterile handling and container technology (such as aseptic packaging), it can even be stored unrefrigerated for 3-4 months.

Pasteurization typically uses temperatures below boiling since at very high temperatures milk, casein micelles will irreversibly aggregate (or 'curdle'). There are two main types of pasteurization used today: High Temperature/Short Time (HTST) and 'Extended Shelf Life (ESL)' treatment. Ultra-high temperature (UHT or ultra-heat treated) is also used for milk treatment. In the HTST process, milk is forced between metal plates or through pipes heated on the outside by hot water, and is heated to 71.7 °C (161 °F) for 15-20 seconds. UHT processing holds the milk at a temperature of 135 °C (275 °F) for a fraction of a second. ESL milk has a microbial filtration step and lower temperatures than HTST. Milk simply labelled 'pasteurised' is usually treated with the HTST method, whereas milk labeled 'ultra-pasteurised' or simply 'UHT' has been treated with the UHT method.

Pasteurization methods are usually standardised and controlled by national food safety agencies (such as the USDA in the United States and the Food Standards Agency in the United Kingdom). These agencies require milk to be HTST pasteurised in order to qualify for the 'pasteurization' label. There are different standards for different dairy products, depending on the fat content and the intended usage. For example, the pasteurization standards for cream differ from the standards for fluid milk, and the standards for pasteurizing cheese are designed to preserve the phosphatase enzyme, which aids in cutting.

The HTST pasteurization standard was designed to achieve a 5-log reduction, killing 99.999 per cent of the number of viable micro-organisms in milk. This is considered adequate for destroying almost all yeasts, mold, and common spoilage bacteria and also to ensure adequate destruction of common pathogenic heat-resistant organisms (including *Mycobacterium tuberculosis,* which causes tuberculosis and *Coxiella burnetii*, which causes Q fever). HTST pasteurization processes must be designed so that the milk is heated evenly, and no part of the milk is subject to a shorter time or a lower temperature.

A growing body of research supports the belief that pasteurization was not so much a response to any hazards or contamination issues with milk itself, but rather may have been a response to the hazards and contamination issues that resulted from the newly emerging 'industrialised' dairy industry. It's likely that, with the burgeoning growth of large-scale, longer-distance distribution networks, the rise of chain-store supermarkets, and the resulting impetus for larger-herd dairy operations and mechanised milking, there came a corresponding inability to preserve the quality and inherent bacterial-resistance qualities of fresh milk being marketed in a localised area.

## Effectiveness of Pasteurization

Milk pasteurization has been subject to increasing scrutiny in recent years, due to the discovery of pathogens that are both widespread and heat resistant (able to survive pasteurization in significant numbers). One of these pathogens, *Mycobacterium avium* subsp. *paratuberculosis* (MAP), is linked to Crohn's Disease. Researchers have developed more sensitive diagnostics, such as real-time PCR and improved culture methods that have enabled them to identify pathogens in pasteurised milk.

Some of the diseases that pasteurization can prevent are tuberculosis, diphtheria, salmonellosis, strep throat, scarlet fever, listeriosis, brucellosis and typhoid fever.

**Food Irradiation**

Food irradiation is the process of exposing food to ionizing radiation to destroy microorganisms, bacteria, viruses, or insects that might be present in the food. Further applications include sprout inhibition, delay of ripening, increase of juice yield, and improvement of re-hydration. Irradiation is a more general term of deliberate exposure of materials to radiation to achieve a technical goal (in this context "ionizing radiation" is implied). As such it is also used on non-food items, such as medical hardware, plastics, tubes for gas-pipelines, hoses for floor-heating, shrink-foils for food packaging, automobile parts, wires and cables (isolation), tires, and even gemstones. Compared to the amount of food irradiated, the volume of those every-day applications is huge but not noticed by the consumer.

The genuine effect of processing food by ionizing radiation involves damage to DNA, the basic genetic information for life. Microorganisms can no longer proliferate and continue their malignant or pathogenic activities. Spoilage-causing micro-organisms cannot continue their activities. Insects do not survive, or become incapable of proliferation. Plants cannot continue the natural ripening or aging process.

The specialty of processing food by ionizing radiation is that the energy density per atomic transition is very high, it can cleave molecules and induce ionization (hence the name), which is not achieved by mere heating. This is the reason for both new effects and new concerns. The treatment of solid food by ionizing radiation can provide an effect similar to heat pasteurization of liquids, such as milk. However, the use of the term 'cold pasteurization' to describe irradiated foods is controversial, since pasteurization and irradiation are fundamentally different processes.

Food irradiation is currently permitted by over 40 countries, and the volume of food so treated is estimated to exceed 500,000 metric tons annually world-wide.

By irradiating food, depending on the dose, some or all of the harmful bacteria and other pathogens present are killed. This prolongs the shelf-life of the food in cases where microbial spoilage is the limiting factor. Some foods, e.g., herbs and spices, are irradiated at sufficient doses (five kilograys or more) to reduce the microbial counts by several orders of magnitude; such ingredients will not carry over spoilage or pathogen microorganisms into the final product. It has also been shown that irradiation can delay the ripening of fruits or the sprouting of vegetables.

Furthermore, insect pests can be sterilized (be made incapable of proliferation) using irradiation at relatively low doses. In consequence, the United States Department of Agriculture (USDA) has approved the use of low-level irradiation as an alternative treatment to pesticides for fruits and vegetables that are considered hosts to a number of insect pests, including fruit flies and seed weevils; the U.S. Food and Drug Administration (FDA) has cleared among a number of other applications the treatment of hamburger patties to eliminate the residual risk of a contamination by a virulent E. coli. The United Nations Food and Agricultural Organization (FAO) has passed a motion to commit member states to implement irradiation technology for their national phytosanitary programmes; the General assembly of the International Atomic Energy Agency (IAEA) has urged to make wider use of the irradiation technology. Additionally, the USDA has made a number of bi-lateral agreements with developing countries to facilitate the imports of exotic fruits and to simplify the quarantine procedures.

The European Union has regulated processing of food by ionizing radiation in specific directives since 1999; the relevant documents and reports are accessible online. The 'implementing' directive contains a 'positive list' permitting irradiation of only dried aromatic herbs, spices, and vegetable seasonings. However, any Member State is permitted to maintain previously granted clearances or to add new clearance as granted in other Member States, in the case the EC's Scientific Committee on Food (SCF) has given a positive vote for the respective application. Presently, six Member States (Belgium, France, Italy, Netherlands, Poland, United Kingdom) have adopted such provisions.

Because of the 'Single Market' of the EC, any food — even if irradiated — must be allowed to be marketed in any other Member State even if a general ban of food irradiation prevails, under the condition that the food has been irradiated legally in the state of origin. Furthermore, imports into the EC are possible from third countries if the irradiation facility had been inspected and licensed by the EC and the treatment is legal within the EC or some Member state.

The Scientific Committee on Food (SCF) of the EC has given a positive vote on eight categories of food to be irradiated. However, in a compromise between the European Parliament and the European Commission, only dried aromatic herbs, spices, and vegetable seasonings can be found in the positive list. The European Commission was due to provide a final draft for the positive list by the end of 2000; however, this failed because of a veto from Germany and a few other Member States. In 1992, and in 1998 the SCF voted 'positive' on a number of irradiation applications that had been allowed in some member states before the EC Directives came into force, to enable those member states to maintain their national authorizations.

In 2003, when Codex Alimentarius was about to remove any upper dose limit for food irradiation, the SCF adopted a 'revised opinion', which in fact was a re-confirmation and endorsement of the 1986 opinion. The opinion denied cancellation of the upper dose limit, and required that before the actual list of individual items or food classes (as in the opinions expressed in 1986, 1992 and 1998) can be expanded, new individual studies into the toxicology of each of such food and for each of the proposed dose ranges are requested. The SCF has subsequently been replaced by the new European Food Safety Authority (EFSA), which has not yet ruled on the processing of food by ionizing radiation.

Other countries, including New Zealand, Australia, Thailand, India, and Mexico, have permitted the irradiation of fresh fruits for fruit fly quarantine purposes, amongst others. Such countries as Pakistan and Brazil have adopted the Codex Alimentarius Standard on Irradiated Food without any reservation or restriction: i.e., any food may be irradiated to any dose.

The measurement of radiation dose is referred to as dosimetry, and involves exposing dosimeters jointly with the treated food item. Dosimeters are small components attached to the irradiated product made of materials that, when exposed to ionizing radiation, change specific, measurable physical attributes to a degree that can be correlated to the dose received. Modern dosimeters are made of a range of materials, such as alanine pellets, perspex (PMMA) blocks, and radiochromic films, as well as special solutions and other materials. These dosimeters are used in combination with specialized read out devices. Standards that describe calibration and operation for radiation dosimetry, as well as procedures to relate the measured dose to the effects achieved and to report and document such results, are maintained by the American Society for Testing and Materials (ASTM international) and are also available as ISO/ASTM standards.

**Low Dose Applications (up to 1 kGy)**

- Sprout inhibition in bulbs and tubers 0.03-0.15 kGy
- Delay in fruit ripening 0.25-0.75 kGy
- Insect disinfestation including quarantine treatment and elimination of food borne parasites 0.07-1.00 kGy

**Medium Dose Applications (1 kGy to 10 kGy)**

- Reduction of spoilage microbes to prolong shelf-life of meat, poultry and seafoods under refrigeration 1.50–3.00 kGy
- Reduction of pathogenic microbes in fresh and frozen meat, poultry and seafoods 3.00–7.00 kGy
- Reducing the number of microorganisms in spices to improve hygienic quality 10.00 kGy

**High Dose Applications (above 10 kGy)**

- Sterilisation of packaged meat, poultry and their products which are shelf stable without refrigeration. 25.00-70.00 kGy
- Sterilisation of Hospital diets 25.00-70.00 kGy
- Product improvement as increased juice yield or improved re-hydration

It is important to note that these doses are above those currently permitted for these food items by the FDA and other regulators around the world. The Codex Alimentarius Standard on Irradiated Food does not specify any upper dose limit NASA is authorized to sterilize frozen meat for astronauts at doses of 44 kGy as a notable exception.

Irradiation treatments are also sometimes classified as radappertization, radicidation and radurization

Gamma radiation is radiation of photons in the gamma part of the electromagnetic spectrum. The radiation is obtained through the use of radioisotopes, generally cobalt-

60 or, in theory, caesium-137. Cobalt-60 is intentionally bred from cobalt-59 using specifically designed nuclear reactors. Caesium-137 is recovered during the refinement of 'spent nuclear fuel', formerly referred to as 'nuclear waste'. Because this technology — except for military applications — is not commercially available, insufficient quantities of it are available on the global isotope markets for use in large scale, commercial irradiators. Presently, caesium-137 is used only in small hospital units to treat blood before transfusion to prevent Graft-*vs*-host disease.

Food irradiation using Cobalt-60 is the preferred method by most processors, because the deeper penetration enables administering treatment to entire industrial pallets or totes, reducing the need for material handling. A pallet or tote is typically exposed for several minutes to hours depending on dose. Radioactive material must be monitored and carefully stored to shield workers and the environment from its gamma rays. During operation this is achieved by substantial concrete shields. With most designs the radioisotope can be lowered into a water-filled source storage pool to allow maintenance personnel to enter the radiation shield. In this mode the water in the pool absorbs the radiation. Other uncommonly used designs feature dry storage by providing movable shields that reduce radiation levels in areas of the irradiation chamber.

One variant of gamma irradiators keeps the Cobalt-60 under water at all times and lowers the product to be irradiated under water in hermetic bells. No further shielding is required for such designs.

### X-ray Irradiation

Similar to gamma radiation, X-rays are photon radiation of a wide energy spectrum and an alternative to isotope based irradiation systems. X-rays are generated by colliding accelerated electrons with a dense material (target) such as tantalum or tungsten in a process known as bremsstrahlungconversion. X-ray irradiators are scalable and have deep penetration comparable to Co-60, with the added effect of using an electronic source that stops radiating when switched off. They also permit dose uniformity. However, these systems generally have low energetic efficiency during the conversion of electron energy to photon radiation requiring much more electrical energy than other systems. Like most other types of facilities, X-ray systems rely on concrete shields to protect the environment and workers from radiation.

Nominal X-ray energy is usually limited to 5 MeV; however, USA has provisions for up to 7.5 MeV which increases the conversion efficiency. Another development is the availability of electron accelerators with extremely high power output, up to 1,000 kW beam. At a conversion efficiency of up to 12 per cent, the X-ray power may reach (including filtering and other losses) 100 kW; This power would be equivalent to a gamma facility with Co-60 of about 6.5 MCi.

## General Economic Aspects

Some foods, particularly fruits and vegetables, are not available for sale on the global market unless treated to prolong shelf life for transportation. This may include radiation processing. However, this application has not yet been exploited. In contrast, irradiation to eliminate insect pests to fulfill quarantine requirements is gaining commercial significance. This is true for fruits Hawaii exports to the U.S. mainland, and increasingly for imports from subtropical countries to the U.S. under bilateral agreements that allows those less-developed countries to earn income through food exports. As an example, Mexico has started to export irradiated guava to the U.S. in 2008, Mango in 2009 and has received approval for Citrus, Star Fruit and Manzano Chili. Furthermore, a number of Asian countries hold bilateral agreements to irradiate exotic fruits for quarantine purposes and export it to the USA.

The actual cost of food irradiation is influenced by dose requirements, the food's tolerance of radiation, handling conditions, i.e., packaging and stacking requirements, construction costs, financing arrangements, and other variables particular to the situation. Irradiation is a capital-intensive technology requiring a substantial initial investment, ranging from $1 million to $5 million. In the case of large research or contract irradiation facilities, major capital costs include a radiation source (cobalt-60), hardware (irradiator, totes and conveyors, control systems, and other auxiliary equipment), land (1 to 1.5 acres), radiation shield, and warehouse. Operating costs include salaries (for fixed and variable labor), utilities, maintenance, taxes/insurance, cobalt-60 replenishment, general utilities, and miscellaneous operating costs.

Treatment costs vary as a function of dose and facility usage. Low dose applications such as disinfestation of fruit range between US$0.01/lbs and US$0.08/lbs while higher dose applications can cost as much as US$0.20/lbs.

## Consumer Perception

Irradiation has not been widely adopted due to an asserted negative public perception, the concerns expressed by some consumer groups and the reluctance of many food producers.

Consumer organizations, environmentalist groups, and opponents to food irradiation refer to some studies suggesting that a large part of the public questions the safety of irradiated foods, and will not buy foods that have been irradiated.

On the other hand, other studies indicate the number of consumers concerned about the safety of irradiated food has decreased in the last 10 years and continues to be less than the number of those concerned about pesticide residues, microbiological contamination, and other food related concerns. The number of people reporting no concerns about irradiated food is among the lowest for food issues, comparable to that of people with no concern about food additives and preservatives. Consumers, given a choice and access to the real irradiated product are ready to buy it in considerably large numbers.

## Labelling and Terminology Issues

Labeling laws differ from country to country. While Codex Alimentarius represents the global standard in particular under the WTO-agreement, member states are free to convert those standards into national regulations. With regard to labelling of irradiated food, detailed rules are published at CODEX-STAN – 1 (2005) labelling of prepacked food.

The provisions are that any 'first generation' product must be labelled 'irradiated' as any product derived directly from an irradiated raw material; for ingredients the provision is that even the last molecule of an irradiated ingredient must be listed with the ingredients even in cases where the unirradiated ingredient will not appear on the label. The RADURA-logo is optional; several countries use a graphical version which differs from the Codex-version.

In the U.S., as in many other countries, irradiated food must be labeled as 'Treated with irradiation' or 'Treated by radiation' and require the usage of the Radura symbol at the point of sale. However, the meaning of the label is not consistent. The amount of irradiation used can vary and since there are no published standards, the amount of pathogens affected by irradiation can be variable as well. In addition, there are no regulations regarding the levels of pathogen reduction that must be achieved. Food that is processed as an ingredient by a restaurant or food processor is exempt from the labeling requirement in the US; other countries follow the Codex Alimentarius provision to label irradiated ingredients down to the last molecule (cf. EU).

FDA is currently proposing a rule that in some cases would allow certain irradiated foods to be marketed without any labeling at all. Under the new rules, only those irradiated foods in which the irradiation causes a material change in the food, or a material change in the consequences that may result from the use of the food, would bear the Radura symbol and the term 'irradiated', or a derivative thereof, in conjunction with explicit language describing the change in the food or its conditions of use. In the same rule FDA is proposing to permit a firm to use the terms 'electronically pasteurized' or 'cold pasteurized' in lieu of 'irradiated', provided it notifies the agency that the irradiation process being used meets the criteria specified for use of the term 'pasteurized'.

Food irradiation is sometimes referred to as 'cold pasteurization' or 'electronic pasteurization' because ionizing the food does not heat the food to high temperatures during the process, as in heat-pasteurization (at a typical dose of 10 kGy, food that is physically equivalent to water would warm by about 2.5 °C). The treatment of solid food by ionizing radiation can provide an effect similar to heat pasteurization of liquids, such as milk. However, the use of the term, cold pasteurization, to describe irradiated foods is controversial, because pasteurization and irradiation are fundamentally different processes, although the intended end results can in some cases be similar.

Consumer perception of foods treated with irradiation is more negative than those which processed using other food processes. 'People think the product is radioactive', said Harlan Clemmons, president of Sadex, a food irradiation company based in Sioux City, Iowa.

## Safety Aspects

### *Safety, Security and Wholesomeness Aspects*

Hundreds of animal feeding studies of irradiated food, including multigenerational studies, have been performed since 1950. Endpoints investigated have included subchronic and chronic changes in metabolism, histopathology, and function of most systems; reproductive effects; growth; teratogenicity; and mutagenicity. A large number of studies have been performed; meta-studies have supported the safety of irradiated food.

Consumer advocacy groups such as Public Citizen or Food and Water Watch maintain that the safety of irradiated food is not proven, in particular long-term studies are still lacking, and strongly oppose the use of the technology.

A report of fatal incidences with pet food in Australia led to some rumours and speculations about the safety of irradiated food and a nationwide recall. In the Australian case 16 cats were reported to have been euthanized after severe paralysis subsequent to being fed a certain cat food The company issuing a recall stated that the problem only occurred with Australian pet-food. The company speculated this was due to irradiating the pet-food. The Australian Quarantine Inspection Services (AQIS) (at that time) required the irradiation to a minimum dose of 50 kGy or heating of imported dry food. After the incident, the pet food manufacturer created a compassion fund for pet owners. The cause of the cat illness is not yet clearly understood and is still under investigation and verification. Vitamin A depletion *wasn't* confirmed in the affected cats. Researchers from Wisconsin University announcing their conference presentation said in the published abstract: *"Here, we show that cats fed an irradiated diet during gestation developed a severe neurologic disease resulting from extensive myelin vacuolation and subsequent demyelination."* There are several Youtube videos claiming to show cats suffering from irradiated food and a video including excerpts from an interview with Dr. Georgina Childs, the veterinarian from SASH involved in the initial cat cases.

## Enforcement of Labelling

There are analytical methods available to detect the usage of irradiation on food items in the marketplace. This may be understood as a tool for government authorities to enforce existing labelling standards and to bolster consumer confidence. The European Union is particularly strict in enforcing irradiation labeling requiring its member countries to perform tests on a cross section of food items in the market-place and to report to the European Commission; the results are published annually in the OJ of the European Communities.

## United States Regulators of Food Irradiation

There has been news that radiation processing of imported cat food has now been banned in Australia. Previously it had been a mandatory requirement for imports including dry and semi-moist food to be irradiated at a minimum dose of 50 kGy or to be heated to a temperature of 100 °C (212 °F) for a minimum of 30 minutes. Actually, the AQIS — having jurisdiction on quarantine issues — has announced with date of 2009-06-06 that the alternative of radiation processing for cat food is no longer acceptable and that irradiated dog food needs to be labeled by 'Must not be fed to cats'. AQIS in its announcement refers to recently published scientific studies and reminds importers of their responsibility to regularly check whether new scientific results could have any implication for their products. This is to say a 'ban' of food irradiation does not exist; and the theory about the causes of ataxia with cats food irradiated products has not been proven. Meanwhile, Dr. G. Child has published a report of the clinical signs and outcomes of those cats. The authors point to epidemiological and to toxicological studies which are still underway. It is not yet clear by which mechanism and what changes induced in the irradiated pet food the damages in the white matter of spinal cord and brain are caused.

## Criticism and Concerns About Food Irradiation

Concerns have been expressed by public interest groups and public health experts that irradiation, as a non-preventive measure, might disguise or otherwise divert attention away from poor working conditions, sanitation, and poor food-handling procedures that lead to contamination in the first place.

A complaint list may contain the following concerns and objections which not all can be covered and discussed in this article:

- food irradiation might be used to mask spoiled food;
- discourage strict adherence to Good Manufacturing Practices;
- preferentially kill 'good' bacteria, encourage growth of 'bad' bacteria;
- devitalize and denature irradiated food;
- impair the flavour;
- not destroy bacterial toxins already present;
- cause chemical changes which are harmful to the consumer.

The Radura logo, as required by U.S. Food and Drug Administration regulations to show a food has been treated with ionizing radiation.

Food irradiation in the United States is primarily regulated by the FDA since it is considered a food additive. Other federal agencies that regulate aspects of food irradiation include:

- United States Department of Agriculture (USDA) — meat and poultry products, fresh fruit.
- Nuclear Regulatory Commission (NRC) — safety of the processing facility.

- United States Department of Transportation (DOT) — safe transport of the radioactive sources.

Each new food is approved separately with a guideline specifying a maximum dosage; in case of quarantine applications the minimum dose is regulated. Packaging materials containing the food processed by irradiation must also undergo approval.

*Note:* The Radura logo as regulated by FDA is slightly different from the international version as proposed in Codex Alimentarius.

'Food irradiation is a pseudo-fix', said Bill Freese, a science policy analyst with the Center for Food Safety in Washington, DC. 'It's a way to try to come in and clean up problems that are created in the middle of the food production chain. I think it's clearly a disincentive to clean up the problems at the source'.

Processors of irradiated food are subject to all existing regulations, inspections, and potential penalties regarding plant safety and sanitation; including fines, recalls, and criminal prosecutions. But critics of the practice claim that a lack of regulatory oversight (such as regular food processing plant inspections) necessitates irradiation. '[Irradiation] is a total cop-out', said Patty Lovera, assistant director of Food and Water Watch. 'They don't have the resources, the authority or the political will to really protect consumers from unsafe food'.

While food irradiation can in some cases maintain the quality (ie. general appearance and 'inner' quality) of certain perishable food for a longer period of time, it cannot undo spoilage which has occurred prior to irradiation. Irradiation cannot be successfully used to mask quality issues other than pathogens. However, as heat pasteurization (example milk), processing by ionizing radiation can contribute to eliminate pathogen risks from solid food (example meat or lettuce). Milk heat-pasteurization is not considered to be a method 'to cover up poor food quality'; consequently, food irradiation should not be accused to serve such criminal purposes . Under a HACCP-concept (Hazard Analysis and Critical Control Point) radiation processing can serve and contribute as an ultimate critical control point before the food reaches the consumer.

Opponents to food irradiation and consumer activists frequently state that the final proof is missing that irradiated food is 'safe' (i.e. not unwholesome). Moreover, the lack of long-term studies should be a further reason not to permit food irradiation. Such questions, by the principle, cannot be answered by science as any scientist should have learned during his studies. Proving the absence of a negative is virtually impossible. For such reasons the basic question needs to be rephrased: What are the chances — the probabilities – that consuming irradiated food will in some way produce unhealthful effects? The scientific consensus is 'very slim'.

A few quick answers to possible questions:

- *Do irradiated foods cause cancer or genetic damage?* It has never happened.
- *Does irradiation change the chemical composition of whatever is irradiated?* Of course it does. That's why it works.

Long-term studies have already been carried on huge numbers of laboratory animals, many species and multiple generations. No negative effects have been observed which could be correlated in a causal way to the irradiation treatment of the food. However, the absence of a noxious effect cannot be proven by the principle, even not in long-term studies. A further complaint is that animal studies cannot be transferred to humans.

There are many more concerns of such kind and the answers have to be found by validating the scientific evidence.

Of course and quite naturally, during the now more than 60 years of research into food irradiation and possibly harmful effects a number of publications have reported such deleterious effects among others as:

- polyploidy in malnourished Indian children
- increase of aflatoxin production by irradiated microorganisms
- vitamin deficiencies at extremely high doses to the complete diet
- non-vitamin effects at higher doses (free radicals?)
- change in chronaxie with rats

However, those experiments could be either not verified in later experiments, could not be clearly attributed to the radiation effect, could be attributed to an inappropriate design of the experiment etc.

In more recent experiments a number of new issues have been raised as:

- possible tumour promoting effect of 2ACBs in extremely high concentrations
- ataxie caused in Australian cats by high-dose irradiated imported feed
- multiple sclerosis caused intentionally in cats by high-dose irradiated feed
- specific effects caused only in pregnant cats by high-dose irradiated feed

In particular, for those very specific situations of those experiments it would be indispensable to defermine whether those animal models have any relevance for human nutrition. Typically, food as intended for human consumption is never irradiated at such extremely high dose levels; on the other hand, feed sterilization by ionizing irradiation is widely accepted standard in rearing of laboratory animals (eg. SPF-free) and in producing gnotobiotic animals for agricultural production.

## Worker Safety and Impact on the Environment

The safety of irradiation facilities is regulated by the United Nations International Atomic Energy Agency and monitored by the different national Nuclear Regulatory Commissions. The incidents that have occurred in the past are documented by the agency and thoroughly analyzed to determine root cause and improvement potential. Such improvements are then mandated to retrofit existing facilities and future design.

Care must be taken not to expose the operators and the environment to radiation or radioactive contamination. Interlocks and safeguards are mandated to minimize this risk. Nevertheless there have been radiation related deaths and injury amongst workers of such facilities, many of them caused by the operators themselves overriding the interlocks. It should be noted that 'ordinary' occupational safety regulations also apply to radiation processing facilities; the radiation aspect are typically excluded and supervised by special authorities.

An incident in Decatur, Georgia where water soluble caesium-137 leaked into the source storage pool requiring NRC intervention has led to near elimination of this radioisotope; it has been replaced by the more costly, non-water soluble cobalt-60.

National and international regulations on the levels and types of energy used to irradiate food generally set standards that prevent the possibility of inducing radioactivity in treated foods, and, hence, excluding the risk to workers and the environment.

## Alternatives

Other methods to reduce several pathogens in food include heat-pasteurization, ultra-high temperature processing, UV radiation, ozone or fumigation with ethylene oxide.

For quarantine purposes, insect pests can also be eliminated by fumigation with methyl bromide or aluminum phosphine, vapour heat, forced hot air, hot water dipping, or cold treatment.

Other methods to extend shelf life of food items include modified atmosphere packaging, carbon monoxide, dehydration, vacuum packaging, freezing and flash freezing as well as chemical additives.

Opponents to food irradiation and consumer activists (cf. Public Citizen maintain that the best alternative to food irradiation to reduce pathogens is in good agricultural practices. For example, farmers and processing plants should improve sanitation practices, water used for irrigation and processing should be regularly tested for E. coli, and production plants should be routinely inspected. Concentrated animal feeding operations near farmland where produce is grown should be regulated.

Proponents of food irradiation have said that practices of organic farming can only reduce the extent of the microorganism load. They assert that residual flora including pathogen germs will always persist; and that processing by ionizing radiation could be the ultimate measure (as a CCP under a HACCP-concept) to practically eliminate such risks.

Farmer Milking a Cow by Hand

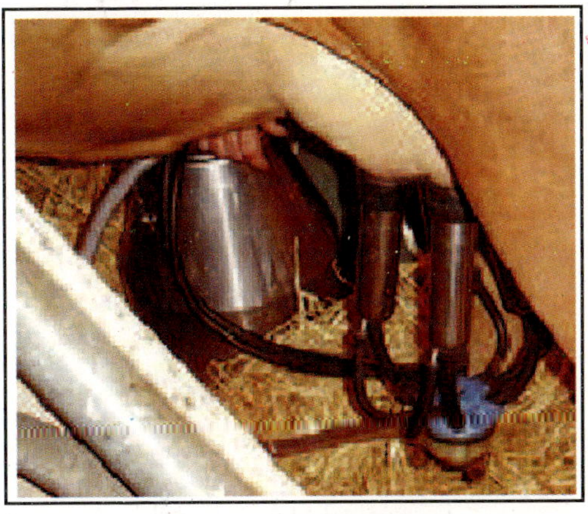

The Milking Machine Extracts Milk from all Teats

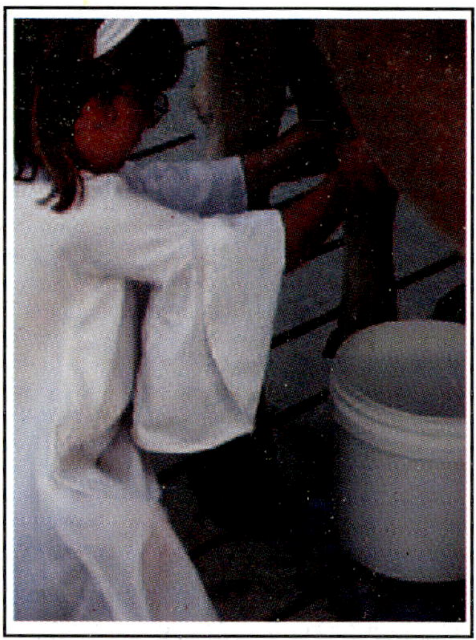

Girl milking a Cow by Hand

A Platter with
Cheese and Garnishes

Feta from Greece

Gouda

A Goat being Milked on an Organic Farm

Cheese Counter at Shop

Churning Cream into Butter using a Hand held Mixer

Mixing Melted Butter with Chocolate to make a Brownie

A Research Flock at U.S. Sheep Experimental Station near Dubois, Idaho

Limburger Cheese

5

# Cheese

Cheese is a generic term for a diverse group of milk-based food products. Cheese is produced throughout the world in wide-ranging flavours, textures, and forms.

Cheese consists of proteins and fat from milk, usually the milk of cows, buffalo, goats, or sheep. It is produced by coagulation of the milk protein casein. Typically, the milk is acidified and addition of the enzyme rennet causes coagulation. The solids are separated and pressed into final form Some cheeses have molds on the rind or throughout. Most cheeses melt at cooking temperature.

Hundreds of types of cheese are produced. Their styles, textures and flavors depend on the origin of the milk (including the animal's diet), whether they have been pasteurized, the butterfat content, the bacteria and mold, the processing, and aging. Herbs, spices, or wood smoke may be used as flavouring agents. The yellow to red colour of many cheeses is from adding annatto.

For a few cheeses, the milk is curdled by adding acids such as vinegar or lemon juice. Most cheeses are acidified to a lesser degree by bacteria, which turn milk sugars into lactic acid, then the addition of rennet completes the curdling. Vegetarian alternatives to rennet are available; most are produced by fermentation of the fungus *Mucor miehei*, but others have been extracted from various species of the *Cynara* thistle family.

Cheese is valued for its portability, long life, and high content of fat, protein, calcium, and phosphorus. Cheese is more compact and has a longer shelf life than milk. Cheesemakers near a dairy region may benefit from fresher, lower-priced milk, and lower shipping costs. The long storage life of some cheese, especially if it is encased in a protective rind, allows selling when markets are favourable.

The word *cheese* ultimately comes from Latin *caseus*, from which the modern word casein is closely derived. The earliest source is from the proto-Indo-European root **kwat-*, which means 'to ferment, become sour'.

More recently, *cheese* comes from *chese* (in Middle English) and *ciese* or *cese* (in Old English). Similar words are shared by other West Germanic languages — West Frisian *tsiis*, Dutch *kaas*, German *Käse*, Old High German *chasi* — all from the reconstructed West-Germanic form **kasjus*, which in turn is an early borrowing from Latin.

When the Romans began to make hard cheeses for their legionaries' supplies, a new word started to be used: *formaticum*, from *caseus formatus*, or 'molded cheese' (as in 'formed', not 'moldy'). It is from this word that we get the French *fromage*, Italian *formaggio*, Catalan *formatge*, Breton *fourmaj* and Provençal *furmo*. *Cheese* itself is occasionally employed in a sense that means 'molded' or 'formed'. *Head cheese* uses the word in this sense.

## Origins

Cheese is an ancient food whose origins predate recorded history. There is no conclusive evidence indicating where cheese-making originated, either in Europe, Central Asia or the Middle East, but the practice had spread within Europe prior to Roman times and according to Pliny the Elder, had become a sophisticated enterprise by the time the Roman Empire came into being.

Proposed dates for the origin of cheesemaking range from around 8000 BCE (when sheep were first domesticated) to around 3000 BCE. The first cheese may have been made by people in the Middle East or by nomadic Turkic tribes in Central Asia. Since animal skins and inflated internal organs have, since ancient times, provided storage vessels for a range of foodstuffs, it is probable that the process of cheese making was discovered accidentally by storing milk in a container made from the stomach of an animal, resulting in the milk being turned to curd and whey by the rennet from the stomach. There is a legend with variations about the discovery of cheese by an Arab trader who used this method of storing milk.

Cheese-making may have begun independently of this by the pressing and salting of curdled milk in order to preserve it. Observation that the effect of making milk in an animal stomach gave more solid and better-textured curds, may have led to the deliberate addition of rennet.

The earliest archaeological evidence of cheese-making has been found in Egyptian tomb murals, dating to about 2000 BCE. The earliest cheeses were likely to have been quite sour and salty, similar in texture to rustic cottage cheese or feta, a crumbly, flavourful Greek cheese.

Cheese produced in Europe, where climates are cooler than the Middle East, required less salt for preservation. With less salt and acidity, the cheese became a suitable environment for useful microbes and molds, giving aged cheeses their pronounced and interesting flavours.

Ancient Greek mythology credited Aristaeus with the discovery of cheese. Homer's *Odyssey* (8th century BCE) describes the Cyclops making and storing sheep's and goats' milk cheese. From Samuel Butler's translation:

> We soon reached his cave, but he was out shepherding, so we went inside and took stock of all that we could see. His cheese-racks were loaded with cheeses, and he had more lambs and kids than his pens could hold...

> "When he had so done he sat down and milked his ewes and goats, all in due course, and then let each of them have her own young. He curdled half the milk and set it aside in wicker strainers".

By Roman times, cheese was an everyday food and cheesemaking a mature art. Columella's *De Re Rustica* (circa 65 CE) details a cheesemaking process involving rennet coagulation, pressing of the curd, salting, and aging. Pliny's *Natural History* (77 CE) devotes a chapter (XI, 97) to describing the diversity of cheeses enjoyed by Romans of the early Empire. He stated that the best cheeses came from the villages near Nîmes, but did not keep long and had to be eaten fresh. Cheeses of the Alps and Apennines were as remarkable for their variety then as now. A Ligurian cheese was noted for being made mostly from sheep's milk, and some cheeses produced nearby were stated to weigh as much as a thousand pounds each. Goats' milk cheese was a recent taste in Rome, improved over the "medicinal taste" of Gaul's similar cheeses by smoking. Of cheeses from overseas, Pliny preferred those of Bithynia in Asia Minor.

Rome spread a uniform set of cheesemaking techniques throughout much of Europe, and introduced cheesemaking to areas without a previous history of it. As Rome declined and long-distance trade collapsed, cheese in Europe diversified further, with various locales developing their own distinctive cheesemaking traditions and products. The British Cheese Board claims that Britain has approximately 700 distinct local cheeses; France and Italy have perhaps 400 each. (A French proverb holds there is a different French cheese for every day of the year, and Charles de Gaulle once asked "how can you govern a country in which there are 246 kinds of cheese?" Still, the advancement of the cheese art in Europe was slow during the centuries after Rome's fall. Many cheeses today were first recorded in the late Middle Ages or after — cheeses like Cheddar around 1500 CE, Parmesan in 1597, Gouda in 1697, and Camembert in 1791.

In 1546, *The Proverbs of John Heywood* claimed 'the moon is made of a greene cheese'. (*Greene* may refer here not to the colour, as many now think, but to being new or unaged.) Variations on this sentiment were long repeated and NASA exploited this myth for an April Fools' Day spoof announcement in 2006.

**Modern Era**

Until its modern spread along with European culture, cheese was nearly unheard of in oriental cultures, in the pre-Columbian Americas, and only had limited use in sub-Mediterranean Africa, mainly being widespread and popular only in Europe and areas influenced strongly by its cultures. But with the spread, first of European imperialism, and later of Euro-American culture and food, cheese has gradually become known and increasingly popular world-wide, though still rarely considered a part of local ethnic cuisines outside Europe, the Middle East, and the Americas.

The first factory for the industrial production of cheese opened in Switzerland in 1815, but it was in the United States where large-scale production first found real success. Credit usually goes to Jesse Williams, a dairy farmer from Rome, New York, who in 1851 started making cheese in an assembly-line fashion using the milk from neighboring farms. Within decades hundreds of such dairy associations existed.

The 1860s saw the beginnings of mass-produced rennet, and by the turn of the century scientists were producing pure microbial cultures. Before then, bacteria in cheesemaking had come from the environment or from recycling an earlier batch's whey; the pure cultures meant a more standardized cheese could be produced.

Factory-made cheese overtook traditional cheesemaking in the World War II era, and factories have been the source of most cheese in America and Europe ever since. Today, Americans buy more processed cheese than 'real', factory-made or not.

## Curdling

A required step in cheesemaking is separating the milk into solid curds and liquid whey. Usually this is done by acidifying (souring) the milk and adding rennet. The acidification can be accomplished directly by the addition of an acid like vinegar in a few cases (paneer, queso fresco), but usually starter bacteria are employed instead. These starter bacteria convert milk sugars into lactic acid. The same bacteria (and the enzymes they produce) also play a large role in the eventual flavour of aged cheeses. Most cheeses are made with starter bacteria from the *Lactococci*, *Lactobacilli*, or *Streptococci* families. Swiss starter cultures also include *Propionibacter shermani*, which produces carbon dioxide gas bubbles during aging, giving Swiss cheese or Emmental its holes.

Some fresh cheeses are curdled only by acidity, but most cheeses also use rennet. Rennet sets the cheese into a strong and rubbery gel compared to the fragile curds produced by acidic coagulation alone. It also allows curdling at a lower acidity — important because flavour-making bacteria are inhibited in high-acidity environments. In general, softer, smaller, fresher cheeses are curdled with a greater proportion of acid to rennet than harder, larger, longer-aged varieties.

## Curd Processing

At this point, the cheese has set into a very moist gel. Some soft cheeses are now essentially complete: they are drained, salted, and packaged. For most of the rest, the curd is cut into small cubes. This allows water to drain from the individual pieces of curd.

Some hard cheeses are then heated to temperatures in the range of 35–55 °C (95-131 °F). This forces more whey from the cut curd. It also changes the taste of the finished cheese, affecting both the bacterial culture and the milk chemistry. Cheeses that are heated to the higher temperatures are usually made with thermophilic starter bacteria which survive this step — either lactobacilli or streptococci.

Salt has roles in cheese besides adding a salty flavor. It preserves cheese from spoiling, draws moisture from the curd, and firms cheese's texture in an interaction with its proteins. Some cheeses are salted from the outside with dry salt or brine washes. Most cheeses have the salt mixed directly into the curds.

Other techniques influence a cheese's texture and flavour. Some examples:

- ❖ *Stretching:* ( Mozzarella, Provolone) The curd is stretched and kneaded in hot water, developing a stringy, fibrous body.
- ❖ *Cheddaring:* Cheddar, other English cheeses) The cut curd is repeatedly piled up, pushing more moisture away. The curd is also mixed (or *milled*) for a long time, taking the sharp edges off the cut curd pieces and influencing the final product's texture.
- ❖ *Washing:* (Edam Gouda, Colby) The curd is washed in warm water, lowering its acidity and making for a milder-tasting cheese.

Most cheeses achieve their final shape when the curds are pressed into a mold or form. The harder the cheese, the more pressure is applied. The pressure drives out moisture — the molds are designed to allow water to escape — and unifies the curds into a single solid body.

**Aging**

A newborn cheese is usually salty yet bland in flavor and, for harder varieties, rubbery in texture. These qualities are sometimes enjoyed — cheese curds are eaten on their own — but normally cheeses are left to rest under controlled conditions. This aging period (also called ripening, or, from the French, *affinage*) lasts from a few days to several years. As a cheese ages, microbes and enzymes transform texture and intensify flavor. This transformation is largely a result of the breakdown of casein proteins and milkfat into a complex mix of amino acids, amines, and fatty acids.

Some cheeses have additional bacteria or molds intentionally introduced before or during aging. In traditional cheesemaking, these microbes might be already present in the aging room; they are simply allowed to settle and grow on the stored cheeses. More often today, prepared cultures are used, giving more consistent results and putting fewer constraints on the environment where the cheese ages. These cheeses include soft ripened cheeses such as Brie and Camembert, blue cheeses such as Roquefort, Stilton, Gorgonzola, and rind-washed cheeses such as Limburger.

### Fresh, Whey and Stretched Curd Cheeses

The main factor in the categorization of these cheese is their age. Fresh cheeses without additional preservatives can spoil in a matter of days.

For these simplest cheeses, milk is curdled and drained, with little other processing. Examples include cottage cheese, Romanian Cas, Neufchâtel (the model for American-style cream cheese), and fresh goat's milk chèvre. Such cheeses are soft and spreadable, with a mild taste.

Whey cheeses are fresh cheeses made from the whey discarded while producing other cheeses. Provencal Brousse, Corsican Brocciu, Italian Ricotta, Romanian Urda, Greek Mizithra, and Norwegian Geitost are examples. Brocciu is mostly eaten fresh, and is as such a major ingredient in Corsican cuisine, but it can be aged too.

Traditional *pasta filata* cheeses such as Mozzarella also fall into the fresh cheese category. Fresh curds are stretched and kneaded in hot water to form a ball of Mozzarella, which in southern Italy is usually eaten within a few hours of being made. Stored in brine, it can be shipped, and is known world-wide for its use on pizzas. Other firm fresh cheeses include paneer and queso fresco.

Categorizing cheeses by firmness is a common but inexact practice. The lines between 'soft', 'semi-soft', 'semi-hard', and 'hard' are arbitrary, and many types of cheese are made in softer or firmer variations. The factor controlling the hardness of a cheese is its moisture content which is dependent on the pressure with which it is packed into molds and the length of time it is aged.

Semi-soft cheeses and the sub-group, *Monastery* cheeses have a high moisture content and tend to be bland in flavor. Some well-known varieties include Havarti, Munster and Port Salut.

Cheeses that range in texture from semi-soft to firm include Swiss-style cheeses like Emmental and Gruyère. The same bacteria that give such cheeses their holes also contribute to their aromatic and sharp flavors. Other semi-soft to firm cheeses include Gouda, Edam, Jarlsberg and Cantal. Cheeses of this type are ideal for melting and are used on toast for quick snacks.

Harder cheeses have a lower moisture content than softer cheeses. They are generally packed into molds under more pressure and aged for a longer time. Cheeses that are semi-hard to hard include the familiar Cheddar, originating in the village of Cheddar in England but now used as a generic term for this style of cheese, of which varieties are imitated world-wide and are marketed by strength or the length of time they have been aged. Cheddar is one of a family of semi-hard or hard cheeses (including Cheshire and Gloucester) whose curd is cut, gently heated, piled, and stirred before being pressed into forms. Colby and Monterey Jack are similar but milder cheeses; their curd is rinsed before it is pressed, washing away some acidity and calcium. A similar curd-washing takes place when making the Dutch cheeses Edam and Gouda.

Hard cheeses — 'grating cheeses' such as Parmesan and Pecorino Romano — are quite firmly packed into large forms and aged for months or years.

## Classed by Content

Some cheeses are categorized by the source of the milk used to produce them or by the added fat content of the milk from which they are produced. While most of the world's commercially available cheese is made from cows' milk, many parts of the world also produce cheese from goats and sheep, well-known examples being Roquefort, produced in France, and Pecorino Romano, produced in Italy, from ewe's milk. One farm in Sweden also produces cheese from moose's milk. Sometimes cheeses of a similar style may be available made from milk of different sources, Feta style cheeses, for example, being made from goats' milk in Greece and of sheep and cows milk elsewhere.

Double cream cheeses are soft cheeses of cows' milk which are enriched with cream so that their fat content is 60 per cent or, in the case of triple creams, 75 per cent.

## Soft-ripened and Blue-vein

There are three main categories of cheese in which the presence of mold is a significant feature: soft ripened cheeses, washed rind cheeses and blue cheeses.

Soft-ripened cheeses are those which begin firm and rather chalky in texture but are aged from the exterior inwards by exposing them to mold. The mold may be a velvety *bloom* of *Penicillium candida* or *P. camemberti* that forms a flexible white crust and contributes to the smooth, runny, or gooey textures and more intense flavours of these aged cheeses. Brie and Camembert, the most famous of these cheeses, are made by allowing white mold to grow on the outside of a soft cheese for a few days or weeks. Goats' milk cheeses are often treated in a similar manner, sometimes with white molds (Chèvre-Boîte) and sometimes with blue.

Washed-rind cheeses are soft in character and ripen inwards like those with white molds; however, they are treated differently. Washed rind cheeses are periodically cured in a solution of saltwater brine and other mold-bearing agents which may include beer, wine, brandy and spices, making their surfaces amenable to a class of bacteria *Brevibacterium linens* (the reddish-orange 'smear bacteria') which impart pungent odors and distinctive flavours. Washed-rind cheeses can be soft (Limburger), semi-hard (Munster), or hard (Appenzeller). The same bacteria can also have some impact on cheeses that are simply ripened in humid conditions, like Camembert.

So-called blue cheese is created by inoculating a cheese with *Penicillium roqueforti* or *Penicillium glaucum*. This is done while the cheese is still in the form of loosely pressed curds, and may be further enhanced by piercing a ripening block of cheese with skewers in an atmosphere in which the mold is prevalent. The mold grows within the cheese as it ages. These cheeses have distinct blue veins which gives them their name, and, often, assertive flavors. The molds may range from pale green to dark blue, and may be accompanied by white and crusty brown molds. Their texture can be soft or firm. Some of the most renowned cheeses are of this type, each with its own distinctive colour, flavour, texture and smell. They include Roquefort, Gorgonzola, and Stilton.

### Processed Cheeses

Processed cheese is made from traditional cheese and emulsifying salts, often with the addition of milk, more salt, preservatives, and food colouring. It is inexpensive, consistent, and melts smoothly. It is sold packaged and either pre-sliced or unsliced, in a number of varieties. It is also available in spraycans.

### Eating and Cooking

At refrigerator temperatures, the fat in a piece of cheese is as hard as unsoftened butter, and its protein structure is stiff as well. Flavour and odour compounds are less easily liberated when cold. For improvements in flavor and texture, it is widely advised that cheeses be allowed to warm up to room temperature before eating. If the cheese is further warmed, to 26-32 °C (79-90 °F), the fats will begin to 'sweat out' as they go beyond soft to fully liquid.

Above room temperatures, most hard cheeses melt. Rennet-curdled cheeses have a gel-like protein matrix that is broken down by heat. When enough protein bonds are broken, the cheese itself turns from a solid to a viscous liquid. Soft, high-moisture cheeses will melt at around 55 °C (131 °F), while hard, low-moisture cheeses such as Parmesan remain solid until they reach about 82°C (180 °F). Acid-set cheeses, including halloumi, paneer, some whey cheeses and many varieties of fresh goat cheese, have a protein structure that remains intact at high temperatures. When cooked, these cheeses just get firmer as water evaporates.

Some cheeses, like raclette, melt smoothly; many tend to become stringy or suffer from a separation of their fats. Many of these can be coaxed into melting smoothly in the presence of acids or starch. Fondue, with wine providing the acidity, is a good example of a smoothly melted cheese dish. Elastic stringiness is a quality that is sometimes enjoyed, in dishes including pizza and Welsh rarebit. Even a melted cheese eventually turns solid again, after enough moisture is cooked off. The saying 'you can't melt cheese twice' (meaning 'some things can only be done once') refers to the fact that oils leach out during the first melting and are gone, leaving the non-meltable solids behind.

As its temperature continues to rise, cheese will brown and eventually burn. Browned, partially burned cheese has a particular distinct flavour of its own and is frequently used in cooking (e.g., sprinkling atop items before baking them).

**Health and Nutrition**

In general, cheese supplies a great deal of calcium, protein, phosphorus and fat. A 30-gram (1.1 oz) serving of Cheddar cheese contains about 7 grams (0.25 oz) of protein and 200 milligrams of calcium. Nutritionally, cheese is essentially concentrated milk: it takes about 200 grams (7.1 oz) of milk to provide that much protein, and 150 grams (5.3 oz) to equal the calcium.

Cheese potentially shares other nutritional properties of milk. The Center for Science in the Public Interest describes cheese as America's number one source of saturated fat, adding that the average American ate 30 lb (14 kg) of cheese in the year 2000, up from 11 lb (5 kg) in 1970. Their recommendation is to limit full-fat cheese consumption to 2 oz (57 g) a week. Whether cheese's highly saturated fat actually leads to an increased risk of heart disease is called into question when considering France and Greece, which lead the world in cheese eating (more than 14 oz/400 g a week per person, or over 45 lb/20 kg a year) yet have relatively low rates of heart disease. This seeming discrepancy is called the French Paradox; the higher rates of consumption of red wine in these countries is often invoked as at least a partial explanation.

Some studies claim that cheddar, mozzarella, Swiss and American cheeses can help to prevent tooth decay Several mechanisms for this protection have been proposed:

- The calcium, protein, and phosphorus in cheese may act to protect.
- Cheese increases saliva flow, washing away acids and sugars.
- Cheese may have an antibacterial effect in the mouth.

## Effect on Sleep

A study by the British Cheese Board in 2005 to determine the effect of cheese upon sleep and dreaming discovered that, contrary to the idea that cheese commonly causes nightmares, the effect of cheese upon sleep was positive. The majority of the two hundred people tested over a fortnight claimed beneficial results from consuming cheeses before going to bed, the cheese promoting good sleep. Six cheeses were tested and the findings were that the dreams produced were specific to the type of cheese. Although the apparent effects were in some cases described as colourful and vivid, or cryptic, none of the cheeses tested were found to induce nightmares. However, the six cheeses were all British. The results might be entirely different if a wider range of cheeses were tested. Cheese contains tryptophan, an amino acid that has been found to relieve stress and induce sleep.

**Lactose**

Cheese is often avoided by those who are lactose intolerant, but ripened cheeses like Cheddar contain only about 5 per cent of the lactose found in whole milk, and aged cheeses contain almost none Nevertheless, people with severe lactose intolerance should avoid eating dairy cheese. As a natural product, the same kind of cheese may contain different amounts of lactose on different occasions, causing unexpected painful reactions. As an alternative, also for vegans, there is already a wide range of different soy cheese kinds available. Some people suffer reactions to amines found in cheese, particularly histamine and tyramine. Some aged cheeses contain significant concentrations of these amines, which can trigger symptoms mimicking an allergic reaction: headaches, rashes, and blood pressure elevations.

**Pasteurization**

A number of food safety agencies around the world have warned of the risks of raw-milk cheeses. The U.S. Food and Drug Administration states that soft raw-milk cheeses can cause "serious infectious diseases including listeriosis, brucellosis, salmonellosis and tuberculosis". It is U.S. law since 1944 that all raw-milk cheeses (including imports since 1951) must be aged at least 60 days. Australia has a wide ban on raw-milk cheeses as well, though in recent years exceptions have been made for Swiss Gruyère, Emmental and

Sbrinz, and for French Roquefort. There is a trend for cheeses to be pasteurized even when not required by law.

Compulsory Pasteurization is Controversial. Pasteurization does change the flavour of cheeses, and unpasteurized cheeses are often considered to have better flavor, so there are reasons not to pasteurize all cheeses. Some say that health concerns are overstated, pointing out that milk pasteurization does not ensure cheese safety. This is supported by statistics showing that in some European countries where young raw-milk cheeses may legally be sold, most cheese-related food poisoning incidents were traced to pasteurized cheeses.

Pregnant women may face an additional risk from cheese; the U.S. Centers for Disease Control has warned pregnant women against eating soft-ripened cheeses and blue-veined cheeses, due to the listeria risk, which can cause miscarriage or harm to the fetus during birth.

Like other dairy products, cheese contains casein, a substance that when digested by humans breaks down into several chemicals, including casomorphine, an opioid peptide. In the early 1990s it was hypothesized that autism can be caused or aggravated by opioid peptides. Based on this hypothesis, diets that eliminate cheese and other dairy products are widely promoted. Studies supporting these claims have had significant flaws, so the data are inadequate to guide autism treatment recommendations.

Although cheese is a vital source of nutrition in many regions of the world, and is extensively consumed in others, its use is not universal. Cheese is rarely found in East Asian dishes, as lactose intolerance is relatively common in that part of the world and hence dairy products are rare. However, East Asian sentiment against cheese is not universal; cheese made from yaks' (*chhurpi*) or mares' milk is common on the Asian steppes; the national dish of Bhutan, *ema datsi*, is made from homemade cheese and hot peppers and cheese such as Rushan and Rubing in Yunnan, China is produced by several ethnic minority groups by either using goat's milk in the case of rubing or cow's milk in the case of rushan. Cheese consumption is increasing in China, with annual sales more than doubling from 1996 to 2003 (to a still small 30 million U.S. dollars a year) Certain kinds of Chinese preserved bean curd are sometimes misleadingly referred to in English as 'Chinese cheese', because of their texture and strong flavour.

Strict followers of the dietary laws of Islam and Judaism must avoid cheeses made with rennet from animals not slaughtered in a manner adhering to halal or kosher laws. Both faiths allow cheese made with vegetable-based rennet or with rennet made from animals that were processed in a halal or kosher manner. Many less-orthodox Jews also believe that rennet undergoes enough processing to change its nature entirely, and do not consider it to ever violate kosher law. As cheese is a dairy food under kosher rules it cannot be eaten in the same meal with any meat.

Rennet derived from animal slaughter, and thus cheese made with animal-derived rennet, is not vegetarian. Most widely available vegetarian cheeses are made using rennet produced by fermentation of the fungus *Mucor miehei*. Vegans and other dairy-avoiding vegetarians do not eat real cheese at all, but some vegetable-based cheese substitutes (usually soy-and almond-based) are available.

Even in cultures with long cheese traditions, it is not unusual to find people who perceive cheese — especially pungent-smelling or mold-bearing varieties such as Limburger or Roquefort — as unpalatable. Food-science writer Harold McGee proposes that cheese is such an acquired taste because it is produced through a process of controlled spoilage and many of the odour and flavour molecules in an aged cheese are the same found in rotten foods. He notes, "An aversion to the odor of decay has the obvious biological value of steering us away from possible food poisoning, so it is no wonder that an animal food that gives off whiffs of shoes and soil and the stable takes some getting used to."

6

# Dairy Cattle

Dairy cattle (dairy cows) are cattle cows (adult females) bred for the ability to produce large quantities of milk, from which dairy products are made. Dairy cows generally are of the species *Bos taurus*.

Historically, there was little distinction between dairy cattle and beef cattle, with the same stock often being used for both meat and milk production. Today, dairy cows are specialized and most have been bred to produce large volumes of milk, with little or no regard for their production of meat. Between 1959 and 1990, US milk production doubled while the number of dairy cows declined 40 per cent.

Dairy cows may be found in herds on dairy farms where dairy farmers own, manage, care for, and collect milk from them. Dairy cow herds range in size from small farms of fewer than five cows to large conglomerates of 25,000 cows or more. The average dairy farmer in the United States manages about one hundred cows but this varies from an average of 800 cows in California to under 80 in the North East states. Herd sizes vary around the world depending on landholding culture and social structure. In many European countries the average herd size is well below 50. In the UK it is over 100 in New Zealand 350 and Australia 280.

To maintain high milk production, a dairy cow must be bred and produce calves. Depending on market conditions, the cow may be bred with a dairy bull or a beef bull. Female calves (heifers) with dairy breeding may be kept as replacement cows for the dairy herd. If a replacement cow turns out to be a substandard producer of milk, she then goes to market. Cross-bred female calves, and all male calves, generally go to market as veal or beef. Most dairy farmers begin breeding heifers as early as fourteen months of age. A cow's gestation period is approximately nine months, so most heifers give birth at around two years of age.

The natural lifespan of a dairy cow is approximately 25 years, however dairy cows are rarely kept longer than five years prior to slaughter. Herd life is strongly correlated with production levels. Lower production cows live longer than high production cows, but are less profitable so are sent for slaughter at a younger age.

Approximately 17 per cent of the US beef supply comes from spent dairy cows: cows who are no longer economically viable for milk production. These animals may be sold due to common diseases of milk cows including mastitis, a bacterial udder infection, foot rot, from standing long periods of time in manure, an inability to stand due calcium depletion from years of intensive milking, and Johne's disease. Johne's disease may be transmissible to humans as Crohn's disease.

The use of spent dairy cows received negative publicity after a Humane Society of the United States undercover video showing a downer cow being illegally mistreated at a California slaughter facility.

In India, the Hindu majority holds the cow as sacred and a motherly figure due to her capacity to give milk. Cow slaughter is legally banned in India (except in the state of Kerala), hence there is no such thing as 'beef cattle' in India. Thus, spent dairy cows don't go to slaughter, but are often seen as roaming on the city streets and die of old age or disease. Some pious Hindu organizations manage 'old age homes' (Hindi: *gaushala*) for old dairy cows.

Market calves are generally sold at two weeks of age and bull calves may fetch a premium over heifers due to their size, either current or potential. Calves may be sold for veal, or for one of several types of beef production, depending on available local crops and markets. Such bull calves may be castrated if turnout onto pastures is envisaged, in order to render the animals less aggressive. Purebred bulls from elite cows may be put into progeny testing schemes to find out whether they might become superior sires for breeding. Such animals may become extremely valuable.

Most dairy farms separate calves from their mothers within a day of birth to reduce bonding. Studies have been done allowing calves to remain with their mothers for 1, 4, 7 or 14 days after birth. Cows whose calves were removed longer than one day after birth showed increased searching, sniffing and vocalizations. However, calves allowed to remain with their mothers for longer periods showed weight gains at three times the rate of early removals as well as more searching behaviour and better social relationships with other calves.

After separation, most young dairy calves subsist on commercial milk replacer, a feed based on dried milk powder. Milk replacer is an economical alternative to feeding whole milk because it is cheaper, can be bought at varying fat and protein percentages. A day old calf consumes around 2 litres of milk per day.

A bull calf with high genetic potential may be reared for breeding purposes. It may be kept by a dairy farm as a herd bull, to provide natural breeding for the herd cows. A bull may service up to 50 or 60 cows during a breeding season. Any more and the sperm count will decline, leading to cows "returning to service" (to be bred again). A herd bull may only stay for one season since over two years old their temperament becomes too unpredictable.

Bull calves intended for breeding commonly are bred on specialized dairy breeding farms, not production farms. These farms are the major source of stocks for AI.

## Milk Production Levels

A cow will produce large amounts of milk over her lifetime. Certain breeds produce more milk than others; however, different breeds produce within a range of around 4,000 to over 10,000 kg of milk per annum. The average for dairy cows in the US in 2005 was 8,800 kg (19,576 pounds).

Production levels peak at around 40 to 60 days after calving. The cow is then bred. Production declines steadily afterwards, until, at about 305 days after calving, the cow is 'dried off', and milking ceases. About sixty days later, one year after the birth of her previous calf, a cow will calve again. High production cows are more difficult to breed at a one year interval. Many farms take the view that 13 or even 14 month cycles are more appropriate for this type of cow.

Dairy cows may continue to be economically productive for many lactations. Ten or more lactations are possible. The chances of problems arising which may lead to a cow being culled are however, high; the average herd life of US Holsteins is today fewer than 3 lactations. This requires more herd replacements to be reared or purchased. Over 90 per cent of all cows are culled for four main reasons:

- *Infertility* — failure to conceive and reduced milk production.

  Cows are at their most fertile between 60 and 80 days after calving. Cows remaining "open" (not with calf) after this period become increasingly difficult to breed, which may be due to poor health. Milk fever, failure to expel the afterbirth from a previous pregnancy, luteal cysts, or metritis, an infection of the uterus, are common.

- ❖ ***Mastitis*** — persistent and potentially fatal mammary gland infection, leading to high somatic cell counts and loss of production.

  Mastitis is recognized by a reddening and swelling of the infected quarter of the udder and the presence of whitish clots or pus in the milk. Treatment is possible with long-acting antibiotics but milk from such cows is not marketable until drug residues have left the cow's system.

- ❖ ***Lameness*** — persistent foot infection or leg problems causing infertility and loss of production.

  High feed levels of highly digestible carbohydrate cause acidic conditions in the cow's rumen. This leads to laminitis and subsequent lameness, leaving the cow vulnerable to other foot infections and problems which may be exacerbated by standing in feces or water soaked areas.

- ❖ ***Production*** — some animals fail to produce economic levels of milk to justify their feed costs.

Production below 12 to 15 liters of milk per day are not economically viable.

Herd life is strongly correlated with production levels. Lower production cows live longer than high production cows, but may be less profitable. Cows no longer wanted for milk production are sent to slaughter. Their meat is of relatively low value and is generally used for processed meat.

## Reproduction

Since the 1950s, artificial insemination (AI) is used at most dairy farms; these farms may keep no bull. Advantages of using AI include its low cost and ease compared to maintaining a bull, ability to select from a large number of bulls to match the anticipated market for the resulting calves, and predictable results.

More recently, embryo transfer has been used to enable the multiplication of progeny from elite cows. Such cows are given hormone treatments to produce multiple embryos. These are then 'flushed' from the cow's uterus. 7-12 embryos are consequently removed from these donor cows and transferred into other cows who serve as surrogate mothers. The result will be between 3 and 6 calves instead of the normal single, or rarely, twins.

Hormone treatments are given to dairy cows to increase reproduction and to increase milk production.

The hormones are used to produce multiple embryos have to be administered at specific times to dairy cattle to induce ovulation. Frequently, for economic considerations, these drugs are also used to synchronize a group of cows to ovulate simultaneously. The hormones Prostaglandin, Gonadotropin Releasing Hormone, and Progesterone are used for this purpose and sold under the brand names Lutalyse, Cystorelin, Estrumate, Factrel, Prostamate, Fertagyl. Insynch, and Ovacyst. They may be administered by injection, insertion or mixed with feed.

About 17 per cent of dairy cows in the United States are injected with Bovine somatotropin, also called recombinant bovine somatotropin (rBST), recombinant bovine growth hormone (rBGH), or artificial growth hormone. The use of this hormone increases milk production from 11 per cent-25 per cent, but also increases the likelihood of cattle developing mastitis, reduction in fertility and lameness. The U.S. Food and Drug Administration (FDA) has ruled that rBST is harmless to people, although critics point out increased levels of insulin-like growth factor 1 (IGF-1) in milk produced using this hormone. The use of rBST is banned in Canada, parts of the European Union, Australia and New Zealand.

In Rajasthan, an indigenous breed called *Tharparkar* exists, named from the Tharparkar District, now in Sindh Pakistan. Another type of dairy cow known as *Nagauri* from

Nagaur District, the bull of which is renowned for its ability to plow fields and run. Traditionally, they used to pull covered wagons, known as *rath*, and in marriages to transport the newlywed couple. They are now a crutch for thriving agricultural and livestock rearing societies of the Thar Desert.

Many other breeds are used nearly exclusively for Beef, or for both dairy and beef purposes.

## Goat

The domestic goat (*Capra aegagrus hircus*) is a subspecies of goat domesticated from the wild goat of southwest Asia and Eastern Europe. The goat is a member of the Bovidae family and is closely related to the sheep: both are in the goat-antelope subfamily Caprinae. There are over three hundred distinct breeds of goat.

Goats are one of the oldest domesticated species. Goats have been used for their milk, meat, hair, and skins over much of the world. In the twentieth century they also gained in popularity as pets.

Female goats are referred to as *does* or *nannies*, intact males as *bucks* or *billies*; their offspring are *kids*. Note that many goat breeders prefer the terms 'buck' and 'doe' to 'billy' and 'nanny'. Castrated males are *wethers*. Goat meat from younger animals is called *kid* or *cabrito*, and from older animals is sometimes called *chevon*, or in some areas "mutton".

The Modern English word *goat* comes from the Old English *gat* which meant 'she-goat', and this in turn derived from Proto-Germanic **gaitaz* (cf. Old Norse and Dutch *geit* 'goat', German *Geiß* 'she-goat', and Gothic *gaits* 'goat'), ultimately from Proto-Indo-European **ghaidos* meaning 'young goat' but also 'jump' (cf. Latin *haedus* 'kid', Old Church Slavonic *zajeci* 'hare', Sanskrit *jihite* 'he jumps'). To refer to the male of the species, Old English used *bucca* (which survives as 'buck') until a shift to *he-goat* (and *she-goat*) occurred in the late 12th century. 'Nanny goat' originated in the 18th century and 'billy goat' in the 19th.

The most recent genetic analysis confirms the archaeological evidence that the Anatolian Zagros are the likely origin of almost all domestic goats today. Neolithic farmers began to keep them for easy access to milk and meat, primarily, also for their dung, which was used as fuel and their bones, hair, and sinew for clothing, building, and tools. The earliest remnants of domesticated goats dating 10,000 before present are found in Ganj Dareh in Iranian Kurdistan. Domestic goats were generally kept in herds that wandered on hills or other grazing areas, often tended by goatherds who were frequently children or adolescents, similar to the more widely known shepherd. These methods of herding are still used today.

Historically, goat hide has been used for water and wine bottles in both traveling and transporting wine for sale. It has also been used to produce parchment.

Most goats naturally have two horns, of various shapes and sizes depending on the breed. While horns are a predominantly male feature, some breeds of goat have horned females. Polled (hornless) goats are not uncommon and there have been incidents of polycerate goats (having as many as eight horns), although this is a genetic rarity thought to be inherited. Their horns are made of living bone surrounded by keratin and other proteins, and are used for defense, dominance, and territoriality.

Goats are ruminants. They have a four-chambered stomach consisting of the rumen, the reticulum, the omasum, and the abomasum.

Goats have horizontal slit-shaped pupils, an adaptation which increases peripheral depth perception. Because goats' irises are usually pale, the pupils are much more visible than in animals with horizontal pupils, but very dark irises, such as cattle, deer, most horses and many sheep.

Both male and female goats have beards, and many types of goat (most commonly dairy goats, dairy-cross boers, and pygmy goats) may have wattles, one dangling from each side of the neck.

Some breeds of sheep and goats look similar, but they can usually be told apart because goat tails are short and point up, whereas sheep tails hang down and are usually longer and bigger — though some (like those of Northern European short-tailed sheep) are short, and longer ones are often docked.

**Reproduction**

In some climates, goats are able to breed at any time of the year. In temperate climates and among the Swiss breeds, the breeding season commences as the day length shortens, and ends in early spring. Does of any breed come into heat every 21 days for 2 to 48 hours. A doe in heat typically flags her tail often, stays near the buck if one is present, becomes more vocal, and may also show a decrease in appetite and milk production for the duration of the heat.

Bucks (intact males) of Swiss and northern breeds come into rut in the fall as with the doe's heat cycles. Rut is characterized by a decrease in appetite and obsessive interest in the does.

In addition to natural mating, artificial insemination has gained popularity among goat breeders, as it allows easy access to a wide variety of bloodlines.

Gestation length is approximately 150 days. Twins are the usual result, with single and triplet births also common. Less frequent are litters of quadruplet, quintuplet, and even sextuplet kids. Birthing, known as *kidding*, generally occurs uneventfully. Right before kidding the doe will have a sunken area around the tail and hip. Also she will have heavy breathing, a worried look, become restless and show great display of affection for her keeper. The mother often eats the placenta, which gives her much needed nutrients, helps stanch her bleeding, and parallels the behavior of wild herbivores such as deer to reduce the lure of the birth scent for predators.

*Freshening* (coming into milk production) occurs at kidding. Milk production varies with the breed, age, quality, and diet of the doe; dairy goats generally produce between 660 to 1,800 L (1,500 and 4,000 lb) of milk per 305 day lactation. On average, a good quality dairy doe will give at least 6 lb (2.7 l) of milk per day while she is in milk. A first time milker may produce less, or as much as 16 lb (7.3 l), or more of milk in exceptional cases. After the 305 day lactation, the doe will 'dry off', typically after she has been bred. Occasionally, goats that have not been bred and are continuously milked will continue lactation beyond the typical 305 days. Meat, fibre, and pet breeds are not usually milked and simply produce enough for the kids until weaning.

## Diet

Goats are reputed to be willing to eat almost anything, except tin cans, and cardboard boxes. While goats will not actually eat inedible material, they are browsing animals, not grazers like cattle and sheep, and (coupled with their natural curiosity) will chew on and taste just about anything resembling plant matter in order to decide whether it is good to eat, including cardboard and paper labels from tin cans. Another possibility is that the goats are curious about the unusual smells of leftover food in discarded cans or boxes.

Aside from sampling many things, goats are quite particular in what they actually consume, preferring to browse on the tips of woody shrubs and trees, as well as the occasional broad-leaved plant. However, it can fairly be said that their plant diet is extremely varied, and includes some species which are otherwise toxic. They will seldom consume soiled food or contaminated water unless facing starvation. This is one of the reasons why goat rearing is most often free ranging, since stall-fed goat rearing involves extensive upkeep and is seldom commercially viable.

Goats prefer to browse on shrubbery and weeds, more like deer than sheep, preferring them to grasses. Nightshade is poisonous; wilted fruit tree leaves can also kill goats. Silage (corn stalks) is not good for goats, but haylage can be used if consumed immediately after opening. Alfalfa is their favourite hay; fescue is the least palatable and least nutritious. Mold in a goat's feed can make it sick and possibly kill it. Goats should not be fed grass with any signs of mold.

The digestive physiology of a very young kid (like the young of other ruminants) is essentially the same as that of a monogastric animal. Milk digestion begins in the abomasum, the milk having bypassed the rumen via closure of the reticular/esophageal groove during suckling. At birth, the rumen is undeveloped, but as the kid begins to consume solid feed, the rumen soon increases in size and in its capacity to absorb nutrients.

**Behaviour**

Goats are extremely curious and intelligent. They are easily trained to pull carts and walk on leads. Ches McCartney, nicknamed 'the goat man', toured the United States for over three decades in a wagon pulled by a herd of pet goats. They are also known for escaping their pens. Goats will test fences, either intentionally or simply because they are handy to climb on. If any of the fencing can be spread, pushed over or down, or otherwise be overcome, the goats will escape. Being very intelligent, once a weakness in the fence has been discovered, it will be exploited repeatedly. Goats are very coordinated and can climb and hold their balance in the most precarious places. Goats are also widely known for their ability to climb trees, although the tree generally has to be on somewhat of an angle. The vocalization goats make is called bleating.

Goats have an intensely inquisitive and intelligent nature: they will explore anything new or unfamiliar in their surroundings. They do so primarily with their prehensile upper lip and tongue. This is why they investigate items such as buttons, camera cases or clothing (and many other things besides) by nibbling at them, occasionally even eating them.

Life expectancy for goats is between 15 and 18 years. An instance of a goat reaching the age of 24 has been reported.

Several factors can reduce this average expectancy, however; problems during kidding can lower a doe's expected life span to 10 or 11, and stresses of going into rut can lower a buck's expected life span to 8 or 10.

## Goats in Agriculture

Goat husbandry is common through the Norte Chico region in Chile, but also produces severe erosion and desertification. Image from upper Limarí River.

A goat is useful to humans either living or dead, first as a renewable provider of milk and fiber, and then as meat and hide. Some charities provide goats to impoverished people in poor countries, because goats are easier and cheaper to manage than cattle, and have multiple uses. In addition, goats are used for driving and packing purposes.

For instance, the intestine is used to make 'catgut', which is still in use as a material for internal human surgical sutures and strings for musical instruments. The horn of the goat, which signifies wellbeing (Cornucopia), is also used to make spoons.

The taste of goat meat is similar to that of lamb meat ; in fact, in the English-speaking islands of the Caribbean, and in some parts of Asia, particularly Pakistan and India, the word 'mutton' is used to describe both goat and lamb meat. However, some feel that it has a similar taste to veal or venison, depending on the age and condition of the goat. The flavour of goat meat is said to be primarily linked to the presence of 4-methyloctanoic and 4-methylnonanoic acid.

It can be prepared in a variety of ways including stewed, baked, grilled, barbecued, minced, canned, fried, curried, or made into sausage. Due to its low fat content, the meat can toughen at high temperatures without additional moisture. One of the most popular goats grown for meat is the South African Boer, introduced into the United States in the early 1990s. The New Zealand Kiko is also considered a meat breed, as is the myotonic or 'fainting goat', a breed originating in Tennessee.

Some goats are bred for milk, which can be drunk raw, although some people recommend pasteurization to reduce bacteria such as *Staphylococcus aureus* and *Escherichia coli*. If the strong-smelling buck is not separated from the does, his scent will affect the milk. Goat's milk is commonly processed into cheese, goat butter, ice cream, cajeta and other products.

Goat's milk can replace sheep's milk or cow's milk in diets of those who are allergic. However, like cow's milk, goat's milk has lactose (sugar), and may cause gastrointestinal problems for individuals with lactose intolerance.

Goat's milk naturally has small fat globules, which means the cream remains suspended in the milk, instead of rising to the top, as in raw cow's milk; therefore, it does not need to be homogenized.

Many dairy goats, in their prime, average 6 to 8 pounds (2.7 to 3.6 kg) of milk daily (roughly 3 to 4 US quarts (2.7 to 3.6 liters)) during a ten-month lactation, producing more after freshening and gradually dropping in production toward the end of their lactation. The milk generally averages 3.5 per cent butterfat. A doe may be expected to reach her heaviest production during her third or fourth lactation. It is also said that 'formula derived from goat's milk is unsuitable for babies who are lactose intolerant as it contains levels of lactose similar to cow's-milk-based infant formulae'.

Goat butter is white because goats produce milk with the yellow beta-carotene converted to a colourless form of vitamin A.

Goat cheese is known as *chèvre* in France, after the French word for 'goat'. Some varieties include Rocamadour and Montrachet.

The Angora breed of goats produces long, curling, lustrous locks of mohair. The entire body of the goat is covered with mohair and there are no guard hairs. The locks constantly grow and can be four inches or more in length. Angora crossbreeds, such as the pygora and the nigora, have been created to produce mohair and/or cashgora on a smaller, easier-to-manage animal. The wool is shorn (cut from the body) twice a year, with an average yield of about 10 pounds.

Most goats have softer insulating hairs nearer the skin, and longer guard hairs on the surface. The desirable fiber for the textile industry is the former, and it goes by several names (down, cashmere and pashmina). The coarse guard hairs are of little value as they are too coarse, difficult to spin and difficult to dye. The cashmere goat produces a commercial quantity of cashmere wool, which is one of the most expensive natural fibers commercially produced; cashmere is very fine and soft. The cashmere goat fiber is harvested once a year, yielding around 9 ounces (200 grammes) of down.

In South Asia, cashmere is called 'pashmina' (from Persian *pashmina*, 'fine wool'). In the 18th and early 19th century, Kashmir (then called Cashmere by the English), had a thriving industry producing shawls from goat down imported from Tibet and Tartary through Ladakh. The shawls were introduced into Western Europe when the General in Chief of the French campaign in Egypt (1799-1802) sent one to Paris. Since these shawls were produced in the upper Kashmir and Ladakh region, the wool came to be known as 'cashmere'.

Goat breeders' clubs frequently hold shows, where goats are judged on traits relating to conformation, udder quality, evidence of high production, longevity, build and muscling (meat goats and pet goats) and fiber production and the fiber itself (fiber goats). People who show their goats usually keep registered stock and the offspring of award-winning animals command a higher price. Registered goats, in general, are usually higher-priced if for no other reason than that records have been kept proving their ancestry and the production and other data of their sires, dams, and other ancestors. A registered doe is usually less of a gamble than buying a doe at random (as at an auction or sale barn) because of these records and the reputation of the breeder. Children's clubs such as 4-H also allow goats to be shown. Children's shows often include a showmanship class, where the cleanliness and presentation of both the animal and the exhibitor as well as the handler's ability and skill in handling the goat are scored. In a showmanship class, conformation is irrelevant since this is not what is being judged.

Various "Dairy Goat Scorecards" (milking does) are systems used for judging shows in the US. The American Dairy Goat Association (ADGA) scorecard for an adult doe includes a point system of a hundred total with major categories that include general appearance, the dairy character of a doe (physical traits that aid and increase milk production), body capacity, and specifically for the mammary system. Young stock and bucks are judged by different scorecards which place more emphasis on the other three categories; general appearance, body capacity, and dairy character.

The American Goat Society (AGS) has a similar, but not identical scorecard that is used in their shows. The miniature dairy goats may be judged by either of the two scorecards. The 'Angora Goat scorecard' used by the Coloured Angora Goat Breeder's Association CAGBA (which covers the white and the coloured goats) includes evaluation of an animal's fleece colour, density, uniformity, fineness, and general body confirmation. Disqualifications include: a deformed mouth, broken down pasterns, deformed feet, crooked legs, abnormalities of testicles, missing testicles, more than 3 inch split in scrotum, and close-set or distorted horns.

According to Norse mythology, the god of thunder, Thor, has a chariot that is pulled by the goats Tanngrisnir and Tanngnjóstr. At night when he sets up camp, Thor eats the meat of the goats, but take care that all bones remain whole. Then he wraps the remains up, and in the morning, the goats always come back to life to pull the chariot. When a farmer's son who is invited to share the meal breaks one of the goats' leg bones to suck the marrow, the animal's leg remains broken in the morning, and the boy is forced to serve Thor as a servant to compensate for the damage.

Possibly related, the Yule Goat is one of the oldest Scandinavian and Northern European Yule and Christmas symbols and traditions. Yule Goat originally denoted the goat that was slaughtered around Yule, but it may also indicate a goat figure made out of straw. It is also used about the custom of going door-to-door singing carols and getting food and drinks in return, often fruit, cakes and sweets. 'Going Yule Goat' is similar to the British custom wassailing, both with heathen roots. The Gävle Goat is a giant version of the Yule Goat, erected every year in the Swedish city of Gävle.

The Greek god, Pan, is said to have the upper body of a man and the horns and lower body of a goat. Pan was a very lustful god, nearly all of the myths involving him had to do with him chasing nymphs. He is also credited with creating the pan flute.

The goat is one of the twelve-year cycle of animals which appear in the Chinese zodiac related to the Chinese calendar. Each animal is associated with certain personality traits; those born in a year of the goat are predicted to be shy, introverted, creative, and perfectionist. See Goat (zodiac).

Several mythological hybrid creatures are believed to consist of parts of the goat, including the Chimera. The Capricorn sign in the Western zodiac is usually depicted as a goat with a fish's tail. Fauns and satyrs are mythological creatures that are part goat and part human. The mineral bromine is named from the Greek word 'br?mos', which means 'stench of he-goats'.

Goats are mentioned many times in the Bible. A goat is considered a 'clean' animal by Jewish dietary laws and was slaughtered for an honored guest. It was also acceptable for some kinds of sacrifices. Goat-hair curtains were used in the tent that contained the tabernacle (Exodus 25:4). On Yom Kippur, the festival of the Day of Atonement, two goats were chosen and lots were drawn for them. One was sacrificed and the other allowed to escape into the wilderness, symbolically carrying with it the sins of the community. From this comes the word "scapegoat". A leader or king was sometimes compared to a male goat leading the flock. In the New Testament, Jesus told a parable of The Sheep and the Goats (Gospel of Matthew 25)..

Christianity has associated Satan with imagery of goats (see Pan (mythology)). A common superstition in the Middle Ages was that goats whispered lewd sentences in the ears of the saints. The origin of this belief was probably the behavior of the buck in rut, the very epitome of lust. The common medieval depiction of the Devil was that of a goat-like face with horns and small beard (a goatee). The Black Mass, a probably-mythological 'Satanic mass', was said to involve a black goat the form in which Satan supposedly manifested himself for worship.

The goat has had a lingering connection with Satanism and pagan religions, even into modern times. The inverted pentagram, a symbol used in Satanism, is said to be shaped like a goat's head. The 'Baphomet of Mendes' refers to a satanic goat-like figure from 19th century occultism.

## Domestic Sheep

Domestic sheep (*Ovis aries*) are quadrupedal, ruminant mammals typically kept as livestock. Like all ruminants, sheep are members of the order Artiodactyla, the even-toed ungulates. Although the name 'sheep' applies to many species, in everyday usage it almost always refers to *Ovis aries*. Numbering a little over 1 billion, domestic sheep are the most numerous species in their genus.Sheep are most likely descended from the wild mouflon of Europe and Asia. One of the earliest animals to be domesticated for agricultural purposes, sheep are raised for fleece, meat (lamb, hogget or mutton) and milk. A sheep's wool is the most widely used of any animal, and is usually harvested by shearing. Ovine meat is called lamb when from younger animals and mutton when from older ones. Sheep continue to be important for wool and meat today, and are also occasionally raised for pelts, as dairy animals, or as model organisms for science. Sheep husbandry is practised throughout the majority of the inhabited world, and has been fundamental to many civilizations. In the modern era, Australia, New Zealand, the southern and central South American nations, and the British Isles are most closely associated with sheep production.

Sheep-raising has a large lexicon of unique terms which vary considerably by region and dialect. Use of the word *sheep* began in Middle English as a derivation of the Old English word *sceap*; it is both the singular and plural name for the animal. A group of sheep is called a flock, herd or mob. Adult female sheep are referred to as ewes, intact males as rams or occasionally tups, castrated males as wethers, and younger sheep as lambs. Many other specific terms for the various life stages of sheep exist, generally related to lambing, shearing, and age.

Being a key animal in the history of farming, sheep have a deeply entrenched place in human culture, and find representation in much modern language and symbology. As livestock, sheep are most-often associated with pastoral,

Arcadian imagery. Sheep figure in many mythologies — such as the Golden Fleece — and major religions, especially the Abrahamic traditions. In both ancient and modern religious ritual, sheep are used as sacrificial animals.

Domestic sheep are relatively small ruminants, usually with a crimped hair called wool and often with horns forming a lateral spiral. Domestic sheep differ from their wild relatives and ancestors in several respects, having become uniquely neotenic as a result of man's influence. A few primitive breeds of sheep retain some of the characteristics of their wild cousins, such as short tails. Depending on breed, domestic sheep may have no horns at all (polled), or horns in both sexes (as in wild sheep), or in males only. Most horned breeds have a single pair, but a few breeds may have several.

Another trait unique to domestic sheep (as compared to wild ovines, not other livestock) is their wide variation in colour. Wild sheep are largely variations of brown hues, and variation with species is extremely limited. Colours of domestic sheep range from pure white to dark chocolate brown and even spotted or piebald. Selection for easily dyeable white fleeces began early in sheep domestication, and as white wool is a dominant trait it spread quickly. However, coloured sheep do appear in many modern breeds, and may even appear as a recessive trait in white flocks. While white wool is desirable for large commercial markets, there is a niche market for coloured fleeces, mostly for handspinning. The nature of the fleece varies widely among the breeds, from dense and highly crimped, to long and hair-like. There is variation of wool type and quality even among members of the same flock, so wool classing is a step in the commercial processing of the fibre.

Depending on breed, sheep show a range of heights and weights. Their rate of growth and mature weight is a heritable trait that is often selected for in breeding. Ewes typically weigh between 45 and 100 kilograms (99 and

220 lb), and rams between 45 and 160 kilograms (99 and 350 lb). Mature sheep have 32 teeth. As with other ruminants, the front teeth in the lower jaw bite against a hard, toothless pad in the upper jaw. These are used to pick off vegetation, then the rear teeth grind it before it is swallowed. There are eight lower front teeth in ruminants, but there is some disagreement as to whether these are eight incisors, or six incisors and two incisor-shaped canines. This means that the dental formula for sheep is either I:0/4 C:0/0 P:3/3 M:3/3, or I:0/3 C:0/1 P:3/3 M:3/3 There is a large toothless gap between the front "biting" teeth and the rear "grinding" teeth.

For the first few years of life it is possible to calculate the age of sheep from their front teeth, as a pair of milk teeth is replaced by larger adult teeth each year, the full set of eight adult front teeth being complete at about four years of age. The front teeth are then gradually lost as sheep age, making it harder for them to feed and hindering the health and productivity of the animal. For this reason, domestic sheep on normal pasture begin to slowly decline from four years on, and the average life expectancy of a sheep is 10 to 12 years, though some sheep may live as long as 20 years.

Sheep have good hearing, and are sensitive to noise when being handled. Sheep have horizontal slit-shaped pupils, possessing excellent peripheral vision; with visual fields of approximately 270° to 320°, sheep can see behind themselves without turning their heads. However, sheep have poor depth perception; shadows and dips in the ground may cause sheep to baulk. In general, sheep have a tendency to move out of the dark and into well-lit areas, and prefer to move uphill when disturbed. Sheep also have an excellent sense of smell, and, like all species of their genus, have scent glands just in front of the eyes, and interdigitally on the feet. The purpose of these glands is uncertain, but those on the face may be used in breeding behaviours. The foot glands might also be related to reproduction, but alternative reasons, such as secretion of a waste product or a scent marker to help lost sheep find their flock, have also been proposed.

Sheep and goats are closely related as both are in the subfamily Caprinae. However, they are separate species, so hybrids rarely occur, and are always infertile. A hybrid of a ewe and a buck (a male goat) is called a sheep-goat hybrid, and is not to be confused with the genetic chimera called a geep. Visual differences between sheep and goats include the beard and divided upper lip unique to goats. Sheep tails also hang down, even when short or docked, while the short tails of goats are held upwards. Sheep breeds are also often naturally polled (either in both sexes or just in the female), while naturally polled goats are rare (though many are polled artificially). Males of the two species differ in that buck goats acquire a unique and strong odor during the rut, whereas rams do not.

The domestic sheep is a multi-purpose animal, and the more than 200 breeds now in existence were created to serve these diverse purposes. Some sources give a count of a thousand or more breeds, but these numbers cannot be verified. Almost all sheep are classified as being best suited to furnishing a certain product: wool, meat, milk, hides, or a combination in a dual-purpose breed. Other features used when classifying sheep include face colour (generally white or black), tail length, presence or lack of horns, and the topography for which the breed has been developed. This last point is especially stressed in the UK, where breeds are described as either upland (hill or mountain) or lowland breeds. A sheep may also be of a fat-tailed type, which is a dual-purpose sheep common in Africa and Asia with larger deposits of fat within and around its tail.

Breeds are also grouped based on how well they are suited to producing a certain type of breeding stock. Generally, sheep are thought to be either 'ewe breeds' or 'ram breeds'. Ewe breeds are those that are hardy, and have good reproductive and mothering capabilities — they are for replacing breeding ewes in standing flocks. Ram breeds are selected for rapid growth and carcase quality, and are mated with ewe breeds to produce meat lambs. Lowland and upland breeds are also crossed in this fashion, with the hardy hill ewes crossed with larger, fast-growing lowland rams to produce ewes called mules, which can then be crossed with meat-type rams to produce prime market lambs. Many breeds, especially rare or primitive ones, fall into no clear category.

Breeds are categorized by the type of their wool. Fine wool breeds are those that have wool of great crimp and density, which are preferred for textiles. Most of these were derived from Merino sheep, and the breed continues to dominate the world sheep industry. Downs breeds have wool between the extremes, and are typically fast-growing meat and ram breeds with dark faces. Some major medium wool breeds, such as the Corriedale, are dual-purpose crosses of long and fine-wooled breeds and were created for high-production commercial flocks. Long wool breeds are the largest of sheep, with long wool and a slow rate of growth. Long wool sheep are most valued for crossbreeding to improve the attributes of other sheep types. For example: the American Columbia breed was developed by crossing Lincoln rams (a long wool breed) with fine-wooled Rambouillet ewes.

Coarse or carpet wool sheep are those with a medium to long length wool of characteristic coarseness. Breeds traditionally used for carpet wool show great variability, but the chief requirement is a wool that will not break down under heavy use (as would that of the finer breeds). As the demand for carpet-quality wool declines, some breeders of this type of sheep are attempting to use a few of these traditional breeds for alternative purposes. Others have always been primarily meat-class sheep.

A minor class of sheep are the dairy breeds. Dual-purpose breeds that may primarily be meat or wool sheep are often used secondarily as milking animals, but there are a few breeds that are predominantly used for milking. These sheep do produce a higher quantity of milk and have slightly longer lactation curves. In the quality of their milk, fat and protein content percentages of dairy sheep vary from non-dairy breeds but lactose content does not.

A last group of sheep breeds is that of fur or hair sheep, which do not grow wool at all. Hair sheep are similar to the early domesticated sheep kept before woolly breeds were developed, and are raised for meat and pelts. Some modern breeds of hair sheep, such as the Dorper, result from crosses between wool and hair breeds. For meat and hide producers, hair sheep are cheaper to keep, as they do not need shearing. Hair sheep are also more resistant to parasites and hot weather.

With the modern rise of corporate agribusiness and the decline of localized family farms, many breeds of sheep are in danger of extinction. The Rare Breeds Survival Trust of the UK lists 22 native breeds as having only 3,000 registered animals (each), and the American Livestock Breeds Conservancy lists 14 as having fewer than 10,000. Preferences for breeds with uniform characteristics and fast growth have pushed heritage (or heirloom) breeds to the margins of the sheep industry. Those that remain are maintained through the efforts of conservation organizations, breed registries, and individual farmers dedicated to their preservation.

Sheep are exclusively herbivorous mammals. Like all ruminants, sheep have a complex digestive system composed of four chambers, allowing them to break down cellulose from stems, leaves, and seed hulls into simpler carbohydrates. When sheep graze, vegetation is chewed into a mass called a bolus, which is then passed into the first chamber: the rumen. The rumen is a 19 to 38-liter (5 to 10 gal) organ in which feed is fermented via a symbiotic relationship with the bacteria, protozoa, and yeasts of the gut flora. The bolus is periodically regurgitated back to the mouth as cud for additional chewing and salivation. Cud chewing is an adaptation allowing ruminants to graze more quickly in the morning, and then fully chew and digest feed later in the day. This is beneficial as grazing, which requires lowering the head, leaves sheep vulnerable to predators, while cud chewing does not.

During fermentation, the rumen produces gas that must be expelled; disturbances of the organ, such as sudden changes in a sheep's diet, can cause potentially fatal conditions such as bloat. After fermentation in the rumen, feed passes in to the reticulum and the omasum; special feeds such as grains may bypass the rumen altogether. After the first three chambers, food moves in to the abomasum for final digestion before processing by the intestines. The abomasum is the only one of the four chambers analogous to the human stomach (being the only one that absorbs nutrients for use as energy), and is sometimes called the 'true stomach'.

Sheep follow a diurnal pattern of activity, feeding from dawn to dusk, stopping sporadically to rest and chew their cud. Ideal pasture for sheep is not lawn-like grass, but an array of grasses, legumes and forbs. Types of land where sheep are raised vary widely, from pastures that are seeded and improved intentionally to rough, native lands. Common plants toxic to sheep are present in most of the world, and include (but are not limited to) oak and acorns, tomato, yew, rhubarb, potato, and rhododendron.

Sheep are largely grazing herbivores, unlike browsing animals such as goats and deer that prefer taller foliage. With a much narrower face, sheep crop plants very close to the ground and can overgraze a pasture much faster than cattle. For this reason, many shepherds use managed intensive rotational grazing, where a flock is rotated through multiple pastures, giving plants time to recover. Paradoxically, sheep can both cause and solve the spread of invasive plant species. By disturbing the natural state of pasture, sheep and other livestock can pave the way for invasive plants. However, sheep also prefer to eat invasives such as cheatgrass, leafy spurge, kudzu and spotted knapweed over native species such as sagebrush, making grazing sheep effective for conservation grazing. Research conducted in Imperial County, California compared lamb grazing with herbicides for weed control in seedling alfalfa fields. Three trials demonstrated that grazing lambs were just as effective as herbicides in controlling winter weeds. Entomologists also compared grazing lambs to insecticides for insect control in winter alfalfa. In this trial, lambs provided insect control as effectively as insecticides.

Other than forage, the other staple feed for sheep is hay, often during the winter months. The ability to thrive solely on pasture (even without hay) varies with breed, but all sheep can survive on this diet. Also included in some sheep's diets are minerals, either in a trace mix or in licks.

Naturally, a constant source of potable water is also a fundamental requirement for sheep. The amount of water needed by sheep fluctuates with the season and the type and quality of the food they consume. When sheep feed on large amounts of new growth and there is precipitation (including dew, as sheep are dawn feeders), sheep need less water. When sheep are confined or are eating large amounts of cured hay, more water is typically needed. Sheep also require clean water, and may refuse to drink water that is covered in scum or algae.

Sheep are one of the few livestock animals raised for meat today that have never been widely raised in an intensive, confined animal feeding operation (CAFO). Although there is a growing movement advocating alternative farming styles, a large percentage of beef cattle, pigs, and poultry are still produced under such conditions. n contrast, only some sheep are regularly given high-concentration grain feed, much less kept in confinement. Especially in industrialized countries, sheep producers may fatten market lambs before slaughter (called "finishing") in feedlots. Many sheep breeders flush ewes and rams with a daily ration of grain during breeding to increase fertility. Ewes are also flushed during pregnancy to increase birth weights, as 70 per cent of a lamb's growth occurs in the last five to six weeks of gestation.

Sheep are prey animals with a strong gregarious instinct, and a majority of sheep behaviors can be understood in these terms. The dominance hierarchy of *Ovis aries* and its natural inclination to follow a leader to new pastures were the pivotal factors in it being one of the first domesticated livestock species. All sheep have a tendency to congregate close to other members of a flock, although this behavior varies with breed. Farmers exploit this behaviour to keep sheep together on unfenced pastures and to move them more easily. Shepherds may also use Herding dogs in this effort, whose highly bred herding ability can assist in moving flocks. Sheep are also extremely food-oriented, and association of humans with regular feeding often results in sheep soliciting people for food. Those who are moving sheep may exploit this behaviour by leading sheep with buckets of feed, rather than forcing their movements with herding.

In regions where sheep have no natural predators, none of the native breeds of sheep exhibit a strong flocking behaviour. Sheep can also become hefted to one particular local pasture (heft) so they do not roam freely in unfenced landscapes. Ewes teach the heft to their lambs, and if whole flocks are culled it must be retaught to the replacement animals.

Escaped sheep being led back to pasture with the enticement of food. This method of moving sheep works best with smaller flocks.

Flock dynamics in sheep are, as a rule, only exhibited in a group of four or more sheep. Fewer sheep may not react as normally expected when alone or with few other sheep For sheep, the primary defense mechanism is simply to flee from danger when their flight zone is crossed. Secondly, cornered sheep may charge or threaten to do so through hoof stamping and aggressive posture. This is particularly true for ewes with newborn lambs.

Sheep can become stressed when separated from their flock members. Sheep can recognize individual human and ovine faces, and remember them for years. Relationships in flocks tend to be closest among related sheep: in mixed-breed flocks same-breed subgroups tend to form, and a ewe and her direct descendants often move as a unit within large flocks.

Sheep are frequently thought of as extremely unintelligent animals. A sheep's herd mentality and quickness to flee and panic in the face of stress often make shepherding a difficult endeavor for the uninitiated. Despite these perceptions, a University of Illinois monograph on sheep found them to be just below pigs and on par with cattle in IQ, and some sheep have shown problem-solving abilities; a flock in West Yorkshire, England allegedly found a way to get over cattle grids by rolling on their backs, although documentation of this has relied on anecdotal accounts. In addition to long-term facial recognition of individuals, sheep can also differentiate emotional states through facial characteristics. If worked with patiently, sheep may learn their names, and many sheep are trained to be led by halter for showing and other purposes. Sheep have also responded well to clicker training. Very rarely, sheep are used as pack animals. Tibetan nomads distribute baggage equally throughout a flock as it is herded between living sites.

## Reproduction

Sheep follow a similar reproductive strategy to other herd animals. A group of ewes is generally mated by a single ram, who has either been chosen by a breeder or has established dominance through physical contest with other rams (in feral populations). Most sheep are seasonal breeders, although some are able to breed year-round. Ewes generally reach sexual maturity at six to eight months of age, and rams generally at four to six months. Ewes have estrus cycles about every 17 days, during which they emit a scent and indicate readiness through physical displays towards rams. A minority of sheep display a preference for homosexuality (8% on average) or are freemartins (female animals that are behaviorally masculine and lack functioning ovaries).

Without human intervention, rams fight during the rut to determine which individuals may mate with ewes. Rams, especially unfamiliar ones, will also fight outside the breeding period to establish dominance; rams can kill one another if allowed to mix freely. During the rut, even normally friendly rams may become aggressive towards humans due to increases in their hormone levels.

After mating, sheep have a gestation period of about five months, and normal labour may take one to three hours. Although some breeds may regularly throw larger litters of lambs, most produce single or twin lambs. During or soon after labour, ewes and lambs may be confined to small lambing jugs, small pens designed to aid both careful observation of ewes and to cement the bond between them and their lambs.

Ovine obstetrics can be problematic. By selectively breeding ewes that produce multiple offspring with higher birth weights for generations, sheep producers have inadvertently caused some domestic sheep to have difficulty lambing; balancing ease of lambing with high productivity is one of the dilemmas of sheep breeding. In the case of any such problems, those present at lambing may assist the ewe by extracting or repositioning lambs. After the birth, ewes ideally break the amniotic sac (if it is not broken during labor), and begin licking clean the lamb. Most lambs will begin standing within an hour of birth. In normal situations, lambs nurse after standing, receiving vital colostrum milk.

Lambs that either fail to nurse or that are rejected by the ewe require aid to live, such as bottle-feeding or fostering by another ewe.

After lambs are several weeks old, lamb marking (the process of ear tagging, docking, and castrating) is carried out. Vaccinations are usually carried out at this point as well. Ear tags with numbers are attached, or ear marks are applied for ease of later identification of sheep. Castration is performed on ram lambs not intended for breeding, although some shepherds choose to avoid the procedure for ethical, economic or practical reasons. Ram lambs that will either be slaughtered or separated from ewes before sexual maturity are not usually castrated. Docking, which is the shortening of a lamb's tail, is practised for health reasons. Objections to all these procedures have been raised by animal rights groups, but farmers defend them by saying they solve many practical and veterinary problems, and inflict only temporary pain.

Sheep may fall victim to poisons, infectious diseases, and physical injuries. As a prey species, a sheep's system is adapted to hide the obvious signs of illness, to prevent being targeted by predators. However, there are some obvious signs of ill health, with sick sheep eating little, vocalizing excessively, and being generally listless. Throughout history, much of the money and labour of sheep husbandry has aimed to prevent sheep ailments. Historically, shepherds often created remedies by experimentation on the farm. In some developed countries, including the United States, sheep lack the economic importance for drugs companies to perform expensive clinical trials required to approve drugs for ovine use. In such instances, shepherds resort to illegal, extra-label usage of drugs approved for other animals. In the 20th and 21st centuries, a minority of sheep owners have turned to alternative treatments such as homoeopathy, herbalism and even traditional Chinese medicine to treat sheep veterinary problems. Despite some favourable anecdotal evidence, the effectiveness of alternative veterinary medicine has been met with skepticism in scientific journals. The need for traditional anti-parasite drugs and antibiotics is widespread, and is the main impediment to certified organic farming with sheep.

Many breeders take a variety of preventative measures to warn off problems. The first is to ensure that all sheep are healthy when purchased. Many buyers avoid outlets known to be clearing houses for animals culled from healthy flocks as either sick or simply inferior. This can also mean maintaining a closed flock, and quarantining new sheep for a month. Two fundamental preventative programmes are maintaining good nutrition and reducing stress in the sheep. Handling sheep in loud, erratic ways causes them to produce cortisol, a stress hormone. This can lead to a weakened immune system, thus making sheep far more vulnerable to disease. Signs of stress in sheep include: excessive panting, teeth grinding, restless movement, wool eating, and wood chewing. Avoiding poisoning is also important, common poisons are pesticide sprays, inorganic fertilizer, motor oil, as well as radiator coolant (the ethylene glycol antifreeze is sweet-tasting).

Common forms of preventive medication for sheep are vaccinations and treatments for parasites. Both external and internal parasites are the most prevalent malady in sheep, and are either fatal, or reduce the productivity of flocks. Worms are the most common internal parasites. They are ingested during grazing, incubate within the sheep, and are expelled through the digestive system (beginning the cycle again). Oral anti-parasitic medicines known as drenches are given to a flock to treat worms, sometimes after worm eggs in the feces has been counted to assess infestation levels. Afterwards, sheep may be moved to a new pasture to avoid ingesting the same parasites. External sheep parasites include: lice (for different parts of the body), sheep keds, nose bots, sheep itch mite, and maggots. Keds are blood-sucking parasites that cause general malnutrition and decreased productivity, but are not fatal. Maggots are those of the bot fly and the blow-fly. Fly maggots cause the extremely destructive condition of flystrike. Flies lay their eggs in wounds or wet, manure-soiled wool, when the maggots hatch they burrow into a sheep's flesh, eventually causing death if untreated. In addition to other treatments, crutching (shearing wool from a sheep's rump) is a common preventative method. Nose bots are flies that inhabit a sheep's sinuses, causing breathing difficulties and discomfort. Common signs are a discharge from the nasal passage, sneezing, and frantic movement such as head shaking. External parasites may be controlled through the use of backliners, sprays or immersive sheep dips.

A wide array of bacterial diseases affect sheep. Diseases of the hoof, such as foot rot and foot scald may occur, and are treated with footbaths and other remedies. These painful conditions cause lameness and hinder feeding. Ovine Johne's disease is a wasting disease that affects young sheep. Bluetongue disease is an insect-borne illness causing fever and inflammation of the mucous membranes. Ovine rinderpest (or *peste des petits ruminants*) is a highly contagious and often fatal viral disease affecting sheep and goats.

A few sheep conditions are transmittable to humans. Orf (also known as scabby mouth, contagious ecthyma or soremouth) is a skin disease leaving lesions that is transmitted through skin-to-skin contact. More seriously, the organisms that can cause spontaneous enzootic abortion in sheep are easily transmitted to pregnant women. Also of concern are the prion disease scrapie and the virus that causes foot-and-mouth disease (FMD), as both can devastate flocks. The latter poses a slight risk to humans. During the 2001 FMD pandemic in the UK, hundreds of sheep were culled and some rare British breeds were at risk of extinction due to this.

Other than parasites and disease, predation is a threat to sheep and the profitability of sheep raising. Sheep have little ability to defend themselves, compared with other species kept as livestock. Even if sheep survive an attack, they may die from their injuries, or simply from panic. However, the impact of predation varies dramatically with region. In Africa, Australia, the Americas, and parts of Europe and Asia predators are a serious problem. In the United States, for instance, over 1/3 of sheep deaths in 2004 were caused by predation. In contrast, other nations are virtually devoid of sheep predators, particularly islands known for extensive sheep husbandry. Worldwide, canids — including the domestic dog – are responsible for most sheep deaths. Other animals that occasionally prey on sheep include: felines, bears, birds of prey, ravens and feral hogs.

Sheep producers have used a wide variety of measures to combat predation. Pre-modern shepherds used their own presence, livestock guardian dogs, and protective structures such as barns and fencing. Fencing (both regular and electric), penning sheep at night and lambing indoors all continue to be widely used. More modern shepherds used guns, traps, and poisons to kill predators, causing significant decreases in predator populations. In the wake of the environmental and conservation movements, the use of these methods now usually falls under the purview of specially designated government agencies in most developed countries.

The 1970s saw a resurgence in the use of livestock guardian dogs and the development of new methods of predator control by sheep producers, many of them non-lethal. Donkeys and guard llamas have been used since the 1980s in sheep operations, using the same basic principle as livestock guardian dogs. Interspecific pasturing, usually with larger livestock such as cattle or horses, may help to deter predators, even if such species do not actively guard sheep. In addition to animal guardians, contemporary sheep operations may use non-lethal predator deterrents such as motion-activated lights and noisy alarms. Sheep were among the first animals to be domesticated by humankind; sources provide a domestication date between nine and eleven thousand years ago in Mesopotamia. Their wild relatives have several characteristics — such as a relative lack of aggression, a manageable size, early sexual maturity, a social nature, and high reproduction rates — which made them particularly suitable for domestication. Today, *Ovis aries* is an entirely domesticated animal that is largely dependent on man for its health and survival. Feral sheep do exist, but exclusively in areas devoid of large predators (usually islands) and not on the scale of feral horses, goats, pigs, or dogs, although some feral populations have remained isolated long enough to be recognized as distinct breeds.

The exact line of descent between domestic sheep to their wild ancestors is presently unclear. The most common hypothesis states that *Ovis aries* is descended from the Asiatic (*O. orientalis*) species of mouflon. It has been proposed that the European mouflon (*O. musimon*) is an ancient breed of domestic sheep turned feral rather than an ancestor, despite it commonly being cited as ancestor in past literature. A few breeds of sheep, such as the Castlemilk Moorit from Scotland, were formed through crossbreeding with wild European mouflon.

The urial (*O. vignei*) was once thought to have been a forebear of domestic sheep, as they occasionally interbreed with mouflon in the Iranian part of their range. However, the urial, argali (*O. ammon*), and snow sheep (*O. nivicola*) have a different number of chromosomes than other Ovis species, making a direct relationship implausible, and phylogenetic studies show no evidence of urial ancestry. urther studies comparing European and Asian breeds of sheep showed significant genetic differences between the two. Two explanations for this phenomenon have been posited. The first is that there is a currently unknown species or subspecies of wild sheep that contributed to the formation of domestic sheep. A second hypothesis suggests that this variation is the result of multiple waves of capture from wild mouflon, similar to the known development of other livestock.

Initially, sheep were kept solely for meat, milk and skins. Archaeological evidence from statuary found at sites in Iran suggests that selection for woolly sheep may have begun around 6000 BC, but the earliest woven wool garments have only been dated to two to three thousand years later. By that span of the Bronze Age, sheep with all the major features of modern breeds were widespread throughout Western Asia. However, one chief difference between ancient sheep and modern breeds is the technique by which wool could be collected. Primitive sheep cannot be shorn, and must have their wool plucked out by hand in a process called 'rooing'. This is because fibers called kemps are still longer than the soft fleece. The fleece may also be collected from the field after it falls out. This trait survives today in unrefined breeds such as the Soay and many Shetlands. Indeed, the Soay, along with other Northern European breeds with short tails, unshearable fleece, diminutive size, and horns in both sexes, are closely related to ancient sheep. Originally, weaving and spinning wool was a handicraft practiced at home, rather than an industry. Babylonians, Sumerians, and Persians all depended on sheep; and although linen was the first fabric to be fashioned in to clothing, wool was a prized product. The raising of flocks for their fleece was one of the earliest industries, and flocks were a medium of exchange in barter economies. Numerous biblical figures kept large flocks, and subjects of the king of Israel were taxed according to the number of rams they owned.

## In Africa

Sheep entered the African continent not long after their domestication in western Asia. A minority of historians once posited a contentious African theory of origin for *Ovis aries*. This theory is based primarily on rock art interpretations, and osteological evidence from Barbary sheep. The first sheep entered North Africa via Sinai, and were present in ancient Egyptian society between eight and seven thousand years ago. Sheep have always been part of subsistence farming in Africa, but today the only country that keeps an influential number of commercial sheep is South Africa. South African sheep producers, in an attempt to deal with the numerous predators of Africa, invented the livestock protection collar, which holds poison at the jugular to sicken or kill predators.

From Southwest Asia, sheep husbandry spread quickly in to Europe. Practically from its inception, ancient Greek civilization relied on sheep as primary livestock, and were even said to name individual animals. Scandinavian sheep of a type seen today — with short tails and multi-coloured fleece — were also present early on. Later, the Roman Empire kept sheep on a wide scale, and the Romans were an important agent in the spread of sheep raising throughout the continent. Pliny the Elder, in his Natural History (*Naturalis Historia*), speaks at length about sheep and wool. Declaring "Many thanks, too, do we owe to the sheep, both for appeasing the gods, and for giving us the use of its fleece.", he goes on to detail the breeds of ancient sheep and the many colours, lengths and qualities of wool. Romans also pioneered the practice of blanketing sheep, in which a fitted coat (today usually of nylon) is placed over the sheep to improve the cleanliness and luster of its wool.

During the Roman occupation of the British Isles, a large wool processing factory was established in Winchester, England in about 50 AD. By 1000 AD, England and Spain were recognized as the twin centers of sheep production in the Western world. As the original breeders of the fine-wooled merino sheep that have historically dominated the wool trade, the Spanish gained great wealth. Wool money largely financed Spanish rulers and thus the voyages to the New World by conquistadors. The powerful *Mesta* (its full title was *Honrado Concejo de la Mesta*, the Honorable Council of the Mesta) was a corporation of sheep owners mostly drawn from Spain's wealthy merchants, Catholic clergy and nobility that controlled the merino flocks. By the 17th century, the *Mesta* held in upwards of two million head of merino sheep.

*Mesta* flocks followed a seasonal pattern of transhumance across Spain. In the spring, they left the winter pastures (*invernaderos*) in Extremadura and Andalusia to graze on their summer pastures (*agostaderos*) in Castile, returning again in the autumn. Spanish rulers eager to increase wool profits gave extensive legal rights to the *Mesta*, often to the detriment of local peasantry. The huge merino flocks had a lawful right of way for their migratory routes (*cañadas*).

Exportation of merinos without royal permission was also a punishable offense, thus ensuring a near-absolute monopoly on the breed until the mid-18th century. After the breaking of the export ban, fine wool sheep began to be distributed world-wide. The export to Rambouillet by Louis XVI in 1786 formed the basis for the modern Rambouillet (or French Merino) breed. After the Napoleonic Wars and the global distribution of the once-exclusive Spanish stocks of Merinos, sheep raising in Spain reverted to hardy coarse-wooled breeds such as the Churra, and was no longer of international economic significance.

The sheep industry in Spain was an instance of migratory flock management, with large homogenous flocks ranging over the entire nation. The management model used in England was quite different but had a similar importance to economy of the British Empire. Up until the early 20th century, owling (the smuggling of sheep or wool out of the country) was a punishable offense, and to this day the Lord Speaker of the House of Lords sits on a cushion known as the Woolsack.

The high concentration and more sedentary nature of shepherding in the UK allowed sheep especially adapted to their particular purpose and region to be raised, thereby giving rise to an exceptional variety of breeds in relation to the land mass of the country. This greater variety of breeds also produced a valuable variety of products to compete with the superfine wool of Spanish sheep. By the time of Elizabeth I's rule, sheep and wool trade was the primary source of tax revenue to the Crown of England and the country was a major influence in the development and spread of sheep husbandry.

An important event not only in the history of domestic sheep, but of all livestock, was the work of Robert Bakewell in the 1700s. Before his time, breeding for desirable traits was often based on chance, with no scientific process for selection of breeding stock. Bakewell established the principles of selective breeding — especially line breeding — in his work with sheep, horses and cattle; his work later influenced Gregor Mendel and Charles Darwin. His most important contribution to sheep was the development of the Leicester Longwool, a quick-maturing breed of blocky conformation that formed the basis for many vital modern breeds. Today, the sheep industry in the UK has diminished significantly, though pedigreed rams can still fetch around 100,000 Pounds sterling at auction.

No ovine species native to the Americas has ever been domesticated, despite being closer genetically to domestic sheep than many Asian and European species. The first domestic sheep in North America – most likely of the Churra breed – arrived with Christopher Columbus' second voyage in 1493. The next transatlantic shipment to arrive was with Hernán Cortés in 1519, landing in Mexico. No export of wool or animals is known to have occurred from these populations, but flocks did disseminate throughout what is now Mexico and the Southwest United States with Spanish colonists. Churras were also introduced to the Navajo tribe of Native Americans, and became a key part of their livelihood and culture. The modern presence of the Navajo-Churro breed is a result of this heritage.

## North America

The next transport of sheep to North America was not until 1607, with the voyage of the *HMS Susan Conant* to Virginia. However, the sheep that arrived in that year were all slaughtered because of a famine, and a permanent flock was not to reach the colony until two years later in 1609. In two decades time, the colonists had expanded their flock to a total of 400 head. By the 1640s there were about 100,000 head of sheep in the 13 colonies, and in 1662, a woolen mill was built in Watertown, Massachusetts. Especially during the periods of political unrest and civil war in Britain spanning the 1640s and 50s which disrupted maritime trade, the colonists found it pressing to produce wool for clothing. Many islands off the coast were cleared of predators and set aside for sheep: Nantucket, Long Island, Martha's Vineyard and small islands in Boston Harbor were notable examples. There remain some rare breeds of American sheep — such as the Hog Island sheep — that were the result of island flocks. Placing semi-feral sheep and goats on islands was common practice in colonization during this period. Early on, the British government banned further export of sheep to the Americas, or wool from it, in an attempt to stifle any threat to the wool trade in the British Isles. One of many restrictive trade measures that precipitated the American Revolution, the sheep industry in the Northeast grew despite the bans.

Gradually, beginning in the 1800s, sheep production in the U.S. moved westward. Today, the vast majority of flocks reside on Western range lands. During this westward migration of the industry, competition between sheep (sometime called 'range maggots') and cattle operations grew more heated, eventually erupting into range wars. Other than simple competition for grazing and water rights, cattlemen believed that the secretions of the foot glands of sheep made cattle unwilling to graze on places where sheep had stepped. As sheep production centered on the U.S.

western ranges, it became associated with other parts of Western culture, such as the rodeo. In modern America, a minor event in rodeos is mutton busting, in which children compete to see who can stay atop a sheep the longest before falling off. Another effect of the westward movement of sheep flocks in North America was the decline of wild species such as Bighorn sheep (*O. canadesis*). Most diseases of domestic sheep are transmittable to wild ovines, and such diseases, along with overgrazing and habitat loss, are named as primary factors in the plummeting numbers of wild sheep. Sheep production peaked in North America during 1940s and 50s at more than 55 million head. Henceforth and continuing today, the number of sheep in North America has steadily declined with wool prices and the lessening American demand for sheep meat.

**South America**

In South America, especially in Patagonia, there is an active modern sheep industry. Sheep keeping was largely introduced through immigration to the continent by Spanish and British peoples, for whom sheep were a major industry during the period. South America has a large number of sheep, but the highest-producing nation (Brazil) kept only just over 15 million head in 2004, far fewer than most centers of sheep husbandry. The primary challenges to the sheep industry in South America are the phenomenal drop in wool prices in the late 20th century and the loss of habitat through logging and overgrazing. The most influential region internationally is that of Patagonia, which has been the first to rebound from the fall in wool prices. With few predators and almost no grazing competition (the only large native grazing mammal is the guanaco), the region is prime land for sheep raising. The most exceptional area of production is surrounding the La Plata river in the Pampas region. Sheep production in Patagonia peaked in 1952 at more than 21 million head, but has steadily fallen to fewer than ten today. Most operations focus on wool production for export from

Merino and Corriedale sheep; the economic sustainability of wool flocks has fallen with the drop in prices, while the cattle industry continues to grow.

Australia and New Zealand are crucial players in the contemporary sheep industry, and sheep are an iconic part of both countries' culture and economy. New Zealand has the highest density of sheep per capita (sheep outnumber the human population 12 to 1), and Australia is the world's indisputably largest exporter of sheep and cattle. In 2007, New Zealand even declared 15 February their official National Lamb Day to celebrate the country's history of sheep production.

The First Fleet brought the initial population of 70 sheep from the Cape of Good Hope to Australia in 1788. The next shipment was of 30 sheep from Calcutta and Ireland in 1793. All of the early sheep brought to Australia were exclusively used for the dietary needs of the penal colonies. The beginnings of the Australian wool industry were due to the vision and efforts of Captain John Macarthur. At Macarthur's urging 16 Spanish merinos were imported in 1797, effectively beginning the Australian sheep industry. By 1801 Macarthur had 1,000 head of sheep, and in 1803 he exported 111 kilograms (245 lb) of wool to England. Today, Macarthur is generally thought of as the father of the Australian sheep industry.

The growth of the sheep industry in Australia was explosive. In 1820, the continent held 100,000 sheep, a decade later it had one million. By 1840, New South Wales alone kept 4 million sheep; flock numbers grew to 13 million in a decade. While much of the growth in both nations was due to the active support of Britain in its desire for wool, both worked independently to develop new high-production breeds: the Corriedale, Coolalee, Coopworth, Perendale, Polwarth, Booroola Merino, Peppin Merino, and Poll Merino were all created in New Zealand or Australia. Wool production was a fitting industry for colonies far from their home nations. Before the advent of fast air and maritime shipping, wool was one of the few viable products that was not subject to spoiling on the long passage back to British ports. The abundant new land and milder winter weather of the region also aided the growth of the Australian and New Zealand sheep industries.

Flocks in Australia have always been largely range bands on fenced land, and are aimed at production of medium to superfine wool for clothing and other products as well as meat. New Zealand flocks are kept in a fashion similar to English ones, in fenced holdings without shepherds. Although wool was once the primary income source for New Zealand sheep owners (especially during the New Zealand wool boom), today it has shifted to meat production for export.

**Animal Welfare Concerns**

The Australian sheep industry is the only sector of the industry to receive international criticism for its practices. Sheep stations in Australia are cited in *Animal Liberation*, the seminal book of the animal rights movement, as the author's primary evidence in his argument against retaining sheep as a part of animal agriculture. The practice of mulesing, in which skin is cut away from an animal's perineal area to prevent cases of the fatal condition flystrike, has been condemned by PETA as being painful and unnecessary. In response, a programme of phasing out mulesing is currently being implemented, and some mulesing operations are being carried out with the use of anaesthetic. The Animal Welfare Advisory Committee to the New Zealand Ministry of Agriculture *Code of recommendations and minimum standards for the welfare of Sheep*, considers mulesing a 'special technique' which is performed on some Merino sheep at a small number of farms in New Zealand.

Most of the sheep meat exported from Australia is either frozen carcases to the UK or is live export to the

Middle East. Shipped on livestock carriers in what has been called crowded, unsafe conditions by critics, live sheep are desired by Middle Eastern nations to meet the requirements of ritual halal slaughter. Opponents of the export — such as PETA — say that sheep exported to countries outside the jurisdiction of Australia's animal cruelty laws are treated with horrendous brutality and that halal facilities exist in Australia to make export of live animals redundant. A few celebrities and companies have pledged to boycott all Australian sheep products in protest.

Sheep are an important part of the global agricultural economy. However, their once-vital status has been largely replaced by other livestock species, especially the pig, chicken, and cow. China, Australia, India, and Iran have the largest modern flocks, and serve both local and exportation needs for wool and mutton. Other countries such as New Zealand have smaller flocks but retain a large international economic impact due to their export of sheep products. Sheep also play a major role in many local economies, which may be niche markets focused on organic or sustainable agriculture and local food customers. Especially in developing countries, such flocks may be a part of subsistence agriculture rather than a system of trade. Sheep themselves may be a medium of trade in barter economies.

Domestic sheep provide a wide array of raw materials. Wool was one of the first textiles, although in the late 20th century wool prices began to fall dramatically as the result of the popularity and cheap prices for synthetic fabrics. For many sheep owners, the cost of shearing is greater than the possible profit from the fleece, making subsisting on wool production alone practically impossible without farm subsidies. Fleeces are used as material in making alternative products such as wool insulation. In the 21st century, the sale of meat is the most profitable enterprise in the sheep industry, even though far less sheep meat is consumed than chicken, pork or beef.

Sheepskin is likewise used for making clothes, footwear, rugs, and other products. Byproducts from the slaughter of sheep are also of value: sheep tallow can be used in candle and soap making, sheep bone and cartilage has been used to furnish carved items such as dice and buttons as well as rendered glue and gelatin. Sheep intestine can be formed into sausage casings, and lamb intestine has been formed into surgical sutures, as well as strings for musical instruments and tennis rackets. Sheep droppings, which are high in cellulose, have even been sterilized and mixed with traditional pulp materials to make paper. Of all sheep byproducts, perhaps the most valuable is lanolin: the waterproof, fatty substance found naturally in sheep's wool and used as a base for innumerable cosmetics and other products.

Some farmers who keep sheep also make a profit from live sheep. Providing lambs for youth programs such as 4-H and competition at agricultural shows is often a dependable avenue for the sale of sheep. Farmers may also choose to focus on a particular breed of sheep in order to sell registered purebred animals, as well as provide a ram rental service for breeding. The most valuable sheep ever sold to date was a purebred Texel ram that fetched £231,000 at auction. The previous record holder was a Merino ram sold for £205,000 in 1989. A new option for deriving profit from live sheep is the rental of flocks for grazing; these 'mowing services' are hired in order to keep unwanted vegetation down in public spaces and to lessen fire hazard.

Despite the falling demand and price for sheep products in many markets, sheep have distinct economic advantages when compared with other livestock. They do not require the expensive housing, such as that used in the intensive farming of chickens or pigs. They are an efficient use of land; roughly six sheep can be kept on the amount that would suffice for a single cow or horse. Sheep can also consume plants, such as noxious weeds, that most other animals will not touch, and produce more young at a faster rate. Also, in contrast to most livestock species, the cost of raising sheep is not necessarily tied to the price of feed crops such as grain, soybeans and corn. Combined with the lower cost of quality sheep, all these factors combine to equal a lower overhead for sheep producers, thus entailing a higher profitability potential for the small farmer. Sheep are especially beneficial for independent producers, including family farms with limited resources, as the sheep industry is one of the few types of animal agriculture that has not been vertically integrated by agribusiness.

Sheep meat and milk were one of the earliest staple proteins consumed by human civilization after the transition from hunting and gathering to agriculture Sheep meat prepared for food is known as either mutton or lamb. "Mutton" is derived from the Old French *moton*, which was the word for sheep used by the Anglo-Norman rulers of much of the British Isles in the Middle Ages. This became the name for sheep meat in English, while the Old English word *sceap* was kept for the live animal. Throughout modern history, 'mutton' has been limited to the meat of mature sheep usually at least two years of age; 'lamb' is used for that of immature sheep less than a year.

In the 21st century, the nations with the highest consumption of sheep meat are the Persian Gulf states, New Zealand, Australia, Greece, Uruguay, the United Kingdom and Ireland. These countries eat 14-40 lbs (3-18 kg) of sheep meat per capita, per annum. Sheep meat is also popular in France, Africa (especially the Maghreb), the Caribbean, the rest of the Middle East, India, and parts of China. This often reflects a past history of sheep production. In these countries in particular, dishes comprising alternative cuts and offal may be popular or traditional. Sheep testicles–called animelles or lamb fries—are considered a delicacy in many parts of the world. Perhaps the most unusual dish of sheep meat is the Scottish haggis, composed of various sheep innards cooked along with oatmeal and chopped onions inside its stomach. In comparison, countries such as the U.S. consume only a pound or less (under 0.5 kg), with Americans eating 50 pounds (22 kg) of pork and 65 pounds (29 kg) of beef. In addition, such countries rarely eat mutton, and may favour the more expensive cuts of lamb: mostly lamb chops and leg of lamb.

Though sheep's milk may be drunk rarely in fresh form, today it is used predominantly in cheese and yogurt making. Sheep have only two teats, and produce a far smaller volume of milk than cows However, as sheep's milk contains far more fat, solids, and minerals than cow's milk, it is ideal for the cheese-making process. It also resists contamination during cooling better because of its much higher calcium content. Well-known cheeses made from sheep milk include the Feta of Bulgaria and Greece, Roquefort of France, Manchego from Spain, the Pecorino Romano (the Italian word for sheep is *pecore*) and Ricotta of Italy. Yogurts, especially some forms of strained yogurt, may also be made from sheep milk. Many of these products are now often made with cow's milk, especially when produced outside their country of origin. Sheep milk contains 4.8 per cent lactose, which may affect those who are intolerant.

Sheep are generally too large and reproduce too slowly to make ideal research subjects, and thus are not a common model organism. They have, however, played an influential role in some fields of science. In particular, the Roslin Institute of Edinburgh, Scotland used sheep for genetics research that produced groundbreaking results. In 1995, two ewes named Megan and Morag were the first mammals cloned from differentiated cells. A year later, a Finnish Dorset sheep named Dolly, dubbed "the world's most famous sheep" in *Scientific American*, was the first mammal to be cloned from an adult somatic cell Following this, Polly and Molly were the first mammals to be simultaneously cloned and transgenic. As of 2008, the sheep genome has not been fully sequenced, although a detailed genetic map has been published, and a draft version of the complete genome produced by assembling sheep DNA sequences using information given by the genomes of other mammals.

In the study of natural selection, the population of Soay sheep that remain on the island of Hirta have been used to explore the relation of body size and colouration to reproductive success. Soay sheep come in several colours, and researchers investigated why the larger, darker sheep were in decline; this occurrence contradicted the rule of thumb that larger members of a population tend to be more successful reproductively. The feral Soays on Hirta are especially useful subjects because they are isolated.

Sheep are one of the few animals where the molecular basis of the diversity of male sexual preferences has been examined. However, this research has been controversial, and much publicity has been produced by a study at the Oregon Health and Science University that investigated the mechanisms that produce homosexuality in rams. Organizations such as PETA campaigned against the study, accusing scientists of trying to cure homosexuality in the sheep. OHSU and the involved scientists vehemently denied such accusations.

Domestic sheep are sometimes used in medical research, particularly for researching cardiovascular physiology, in areas such as hypertension and heart failure. Pregnant sheep are also a useful model for human pregnancy, and have been used to investigate the effects on fetal development of malnutrition and hypoxia. In behavioural sciences, sheep have been used in isolated cases for the study of facial recognition, as their mental process of recognition is qualitatively similar to humans.

## Cultural Impact

Sheep have had a strong presence in many cultures, especially in areas where they form the most common type of livestock. In the English language, to call someone a sheep or ovine may allude that they are timid and easily led, if not outright stupid. In contradiction to this image, male sheep are often used as symbols of virility and power, such as for the St. Louis Rams and the Dodge Ram. Sheep are key symbols in fables and nursery rhymes like *The Wolf in Sheep's Clothing*, *Little Bo Peep*, *Baa, Baa, Black Sheep*, and *Mary Had a Little Lamb*. Novels such as George Orwell's *Animal Farm*, Haruki Murakami's *A Wild Sheep Chase*, Thomas Hardy's *Far from the Madding Crowd* and *Three Bags Full: A Sheep Detective Story* utilize sheep as characters or plot devices. Poems like William Blake's 'The Lamb', songs such as Pink Floyd's *Sheep* and Bach's aria *Sheep may safely graze* (*Schafe können sicher weiden*) use sheep for metaphorical purposes. In more recent popular culture, the 2007 film *Black Sheep* exploits sheep for horror and comedic effect, ironically turning them into blood-thirsty killers.

Counting sheep is popularly said to be an aid to sleep, and some ancient systems of counting sheep persist today. Sheep also enter in colloquial sayings and idiom frequently with such phrases as 'black sheep'. To call an individual a black sheep implies that they are an odd or disreputable member of a group. This usage derives from the recessive trait that causes an occasional black lamb to be born in to an entirely white flock. These black sheep were considered undesirable by shepherds, as black wool is not as commercially viable as white wool. Citizens who accept overbearing governments have been referred to by the Portmanteau neologism of sheeple. Somewhat differently, the adjective 'sheepish' is also used to describe embarrassment.

## In Religion and Folklore

In antiquity, symbolism involving sheep cropped up in religions in the ancient Near East, the Mideast, and the Mediterranean area: Çatalhöyük, ancient Egyptian religion, the Cana'anite and Phoenician tradition, Judaism, Greek religion, and others. Religious symbolism and ritual involving sheep began with some of the first known faiths: skulls of rams (along with bulls) occupied central placement in shrines at the Çatalhöyük settlement in 8,000 BCE In Ancient

Egyptian religion, the ram was the symbol of several gods: Khnum, Heryshaf and Amun (in his incarnation as a god of fertility). Other deities occasionally shown with ram features include: the goddess Ishtar, the Phoenician god Baal-Hamon, and the Babylonian god Ea-Oannes. In Madagascar, sheep were not eaten as they were believed to be incarnations of the souls of ancestors.

There are also many ancient Greek references to sheep: that of Chrysomallos, the golden-fleeced ram, continuing to be told through into the modern era. Astrologically, *Aries*, the ram, is the first sign of the classical Greek zodiac and the sheep is also the eighth of the twelve animals associated with the 12-year cycle of in the Chinese zodiac, related to the Chinese calendar. In Mongolia, shagai are an ancient form of dice made from the cuboid bones of sheep that are often used for fortune telling purposes.

Sheep play an important role in all the Abrahamic faiths; Abraham, Isaac, Jacob, Moses, Muhammad and King David were all shepherds. According to the story of the Binding of Isaac, a ram is sacrificed as a substitute for Isaac after an angel stays Abraham's hand. Eid al-Adha is a major annual festival in Islam in which sheep (or other animals) are sacrificed in remembrance of this act. Sheep are also occasionally sacrificed to commemorate important secular events in Islamic cultures. Greeks and Romans also sacrificed sheep regularly in religious practice, and Judaism also once sacrificed sheep as a Korban (sacrifice), such as the Passover lamb. Ovine symbols—such as the ceremonial blowing of a shofar—still find a presence in modern Judaic traditions. Followers of Christianity are collectively often referred to as a flock, with Christ as the Good Shepherd, and sheep are an element in the Christian iconography of the birth of Jesus. Some Christian saints are considered patrons of shepherds, and even of sheep themselves. Christ is also portrayed as the Sacrificial lamb of God (*Agnus Dei*) and Easter celebrations in Greece and Romania traditionally feature a meal of Paschal lamb.

7

# Butter

Butter is a dairy product made by churning fresh or fermented cream or milk. It is generally used as a spread and a condiment, as well as in cooking applications such as baking, sauce making, and frying. Butter consists of butterfat, water and milk proteins.

Most frequently made from cows' milk, butter can also be manufactured from the milk of other mammals, including sheep, goats, buffalo, and yaks. Salt, flavourings and preservatives are sometimes added to butter. Rendering butter produces clarified butter or *ghee*, which is almost entirely butterfat.

Butter is an emulsion which remains a solid when refrigerated, but softens to a spreadable consistency at room temperature, and melts to a thin liquid consistency at 32-35°C (90-95°F). The density of butter is 911 kg/m$^3$ (1535.5 lb/yd$^3$).

It generally has a pale yellow colour, but varies from deep yellow to nearly white. Its colour is dependent on the animal's feed and is commonly manipulated with food colourings in the commercial manufacturing process, most commonly annatto or carotene.

The word *butter* derives (via Germanic languages) from the Latin *butyrum*, which is borrowed from the Greek *boutyron*. This may have been a construction meaning 'cow-cheese' (*bous* 'ox, cow' + *tyros* 'cheese'), or the word may have been borrowed from another language, possibly Scythian. The root word persists in the name butyric acid, a compound found in rancid butter and dairy products such as Parmesan cheese. (Another possibility may be an extended derivation from Sanskrit *bhutari*, meaning 'the enemy of evil spirits'.)

In general use, the term 'butter' refers to the spread dairy product when unqualified by other descriptors. The word commonly is used to describe puréed vegetable or nut products such as peanut butter and almond butter. It is often applied to spread fruit products such as apple butter. Fats such as cocoa butter and shea butter that remain solid at room temperature are also known as 'butters'. In addition to the act of applying butter being called 'to butter', non-dairy items that have a dairy butter consistency may use 'butter' to call that consistency to mind, including food items such as maple butter and Witch's butter and non-food items such as baby bottom butter, hyena butter, and rock butter.

## Production

Unhomogenized milk and cream contain butterfat in microscopic globules. These globules are surrounded by membranes made of phospholipids (fatty acid emulsifiers) and proteins, which prevent the fat in milk from pooling together into a single mass. Butter is produced by agitating cream, which damages these membranes and allows the milk fats to conjoin, separating from the other parts of the cream. Variations in the production method will create butters with different consistencies, mostly due to the butterfat composition in the finished product. Butter contains fat in three separate forms: free butterfat, butterfat crystals, and undamaged fat globules. In the finished product, different proportions of these forms result in different consistencies within the butter; butters with many crystals are harder than butters dominated by free fats.Churning produces small butter grains floating in the water-based portion of the cream. This watery liquid is called buttermilk—although the buttermilk most common today is instead a directly fermented skimmed milk. The buttermilk is drained off; sometimes more buttermilk is removed by rinsing the grains with water. Then the grains are 'worked': pressed and kneaded together. When prepared manually, this is done using wooden boards called scotch hands. This consolidates the butter into a solid mass and breaks up embedded pockets of buttermilk or water into tiny droplets. Commercial butter is about 80 per cent butterfat and 15 per cent water; traditionally-made butter may have as little as 65 per cent fat and 30 per cent water. Butterfat consists of many moderate-sized, saturated hydrocarbon chain fatty acids. It is a triglyceride, an ester derived from glycerol and three fatty acid groups. Butter becomes rancid when these chains break down into smaller components, like butyric acid and diacetyl. The density of butter is 0.911 $g/cm^3$ (527 $oz/in^3$), about the same as ice.

Before modern factory butter making, cream was usually collected from several milkings and was therefore several days old and somewhat fermented by the time it was made into butter. Butter made from a fermented cream is known as cultured butter. During fermentation, the cream naturally sours as bacteria convert milk sugars into lactic acid. The fermentation process produces additional aroma compounds, including diacetyl, which makes for a fuller-flavoured and more 'buttery' tasting product. Today, cultured butter is usually made from pasteurized cream whose fermentation is produced by the introduction of *Lactococcus* and *Leuconostoc* bacteria.

Another method for producing cultured butter, developed in the early 1970s, is to produce butter from fresh cream and then incorporate bacterial cultures and lactic acid.

Using this method, the cultured butter flavour grows as the butter is aged in cold storage. For manufacturers, this method is more efficient since aging the cream used to make butter takes significantly more space than simply storing the finished butter product. A method to make an artificial simulation of cultured butter is to add lactic acid and flavour compounds directly to the fresh-cream butter; while this more efficient process is claimed to simulate the taste of cultured butter, the product produced is not cultured but is instead flavoured.

Dairy products are often pasteurized during production to kill pathogenic bacteria and other microbes. Butter made from pasteurized fresh cream is called sweet cream butter. Production of sweet cream butter first became common in the 19th century, with the development of refrigeration and the mechanical cream separator. Butter made from fresh or cultured unpasteurized cream is called raw cream butter. Raw cream butter has a 'cleaner' cream flavour, without the cooked-milk notes that pasteurization introduces.

Throughout Continental Europe, cultured butter is preferred, while sweet cream butter dominates in the United States and the United Kingdom. Therefore, cultured butter is sometimes labelled *European-style butter* in the United States. Commercial raw cream butter is virtually unheard-of in the United States. Raw cream butter is generally only found made at home by consumers who have purchased raw whole milk directly from dairy farmers, skimmed the cream themselves, and made butter with it. It is rare in Europe as well.

Several spreadable butters have been developed; these remain softer at colder temperatures and are therefore easier to use directly out of refrigeration. Some modify the make-up of the butter's fat through chemical manipulation of the finished product, some through manipulation of the cattle's feed, and some by incorporating vegetable oils into the butter. Whipped butter, another product designed to be more spreadable, is aerated via the incorporation of nitrogen gas–normal air is not used, because doing so would encourage oxidation and rancidity.

All categories of butter are sold either in salted and unsalted forms. Either granular salt or a strong brine are added to salted butter during processing. In addition to enhanced flavour, the addition of salt acts as a preservative.

The amount of butterfat in the finished product is a vital aspect of production. In the United States, products sold as 'butter' are required to contain a minimum of 80 per cent butterfat; in practice most American butters contain only slightly more than that, averaging around 81 per cent butterfat. European butters generally have a higher ratio, which may extend up to 85 per cent.

Clarified butter is butter with almost all of its water and milk solids removed, leaving almost-pure butterfat. Clarified butter is made by heating butter to its melting point and then allowing it to cool off; after settling, the remaining components separate by density. At the top, whey proteins form a skin which is removed, and the resulting butterfat is then poured off from the mixture of water and casein proteins that settle to the bottom.

Ghee is clarified butter which is brought to higher temperatures of around 120 °C (250 °F) once the water has cooked off, allowing the milk solids to brown. This process flavours the ghee, and also produces antioxidants which help protect it longer from rancidity. Because of this, ghee can keep for six to eight months under normal conditions.

Cream may be skimmed from whey instead of milk, as a by-product of cheese making. Whey butter may be made from whey cream. Whey cream and butter have a lower fat content and taste more salty, tangy and 'cheesy'. They are also cheaper than 'sweet' cream and butter.

Since even accidental agitation can form butter from cream, it is likely that its invention dates from the earliest days of dairying, perhaps in the Mesopotamian area between 9000 and 8000 BCE. The earliest butter would have been from sheep or goat's milk; cattle are not thought to have been domesticated for another thousand years. An ancient method of butter making, still used today in parts of Africa and the Near East, involves a goat skin half filled with milk, and inflated with air before being sealed. The skin is then hung with ropes on a tripod of sticks, and rocked until the movement leads to the formation of butter.

Butter was known in the classical Mediterranean civilizations, but it does not seem to have been a common food. In the Mediterranean climate, unclarified butter spoils quickly – unlike cheese it is not a practical method of preserving the nutrients of milk. The ancient Greeks and Romans seemed to have considered butter a food fit more for the northern barbarians. A play by the Greek comic poet Anaxandrides refers to Thracians as *boutyrophagoi*; 'butter-eaters'. In *Natural History*, Pliny the Elder calls butter 'the most delicate of food among barbarous nations', and goes on to describe its medicinal properties. Later, the physician Galen also described butter as a medicinal agent only.

Historian and linguist Andrew Dalby says that most references to butter in ancient Near Eastern texts should more correctly be translated as ghee. Ghee is mentioned in the Periplus of the Erythraean Sea as a typical trade article around the 1st century CE Arabian Sea, and Roman geographer Strabo describes it as a commodity of Arabia and Sudan. In India, ghee has been a symbol of purity and an offering to the gods—especially Agni, the Hindu god of fire—for more than 3000 years; references to ghee's sacred nature appear numerous times in the Rig Veda, circa 1500-1200 BCE. The tale of the child Krishna stealing butter remains a popular children's story in India today. Since India's prehistory, ghee has been both a staple food and used for ceremonial purposes such as fueling holy lamps and funeral pyres.

## Middle Ages

The cooler climates of northern Europe allowed butter to be stored for a longer period before it spoiled. Scandinavia has the oldest tradition in Europe of butter export trade, dating at least to the 12th century. After the fall of Rome and through much of the Middle Ages, butter was a common food across most of Europe, but one with a low reputation, and was consumed principally by peasants. Butter slowly became more accepted by the upper class, notably when the early 16th century Roman Catholic Church allowed its consumption during Lent. Bread and butter became common fare among the middle class and the English, in particular, gained a reputation for their liberal use of melted butter as a sauce with meat and vegetables.

In antiquity, Butter was used for fuel in lamps as a substitute for oil. The *Butter Tower* of Rouen Cathedral was erected in the early 16th century when Archbishop Georges d'Amboise authorized the burning of butter instead of oil, which was scarce at the time, during Lent.

Across northern Europe, butter was sometimes treated in a manner unheard-of today: it was packed into barrels (firkins) and buried in peat bogs, perhaps for years. Such 'bog butter' would develop a strong flavor as it aged, but remain edible, in large part because of the unique cool, airless, antiseptic and acidic environment of a peat bog. Firkins of such buried butter are a common archaeological find in Ireland; the Irish National Museum has some containing "a grayish cheese-like substance, partially hardened, not much like butter, and quite free from putrefaction." The practice was most common in Ireland in the 11th-14th centuries; it ended entirely before the 19th century.

Like Ireland, France became well-known for its butter, particularly in Normandy and Brittany. By the 1860s, butter had become so in demand in France that Emperor Napoleon III offered prize money for an inexpensive substitute to supplement France's inadequate butter supplies. A French chemist claimed the prize with the invention of margarine in 1869. The first margarine was beef tallow flavoured with milk and worked like butter; vegetable margarine followed after the development of hydrogenated oils around 1900.

Until the 19th century, the vast majority of butter was made by hand, on farms. The first butter factories appeared in the United States in the early 1860s, after the successful introduction of cheese factories a decade earlier. In the late 1870s, the centrifugal cream separator was introduced, marketed most successfully by Swedish engineer Carl Gustaf Patrik de Laval. This dramatically sped up the butter-making process by eliminating the slow step of letting cream naturally rise to the top of milk. Initially, whole milk was shipped to the butter factories, and the cream separation took place there. Soon, though, cream-separation technology became small and inexpensive enough to introduce an additional efficiency: the separation was accomplished on the farm, and the cream alone shipped to the factory. By 1900, more than half the butter produced in the United States was factory made; Europe followed suit shortly after.

In 1920, Otto Hunziker authored *The Butter Industry, Prepared for Factory, School and Laboratory*, a well-known text in the industry that enjoyed at least three editions (1920, 1927, 1940). As part of the efforts of the American Dairy Science Association, Professor Hunziker and others published articles regarding: causes of tallowiness (an odor defect, distinct from rancidity, a taste defect); mottles (an aesthetic issue related to uneven colour); introduced salts; the impact of creamery metals and liquids; and acidity measurement. These and other ADSA publications helped standardize practices internationally.

Per capita butter consumption declined in most western nations during the 20th century, in large part because of the rising popularity of margarine, which is less expensive and, until recent years, was perceived as being healthier. In the

United States, margarine consumption overtook butter during the 1950s and it is still the case today that more margarine than butter is eaten in the U.S. and the EU.

Due to historical variances in butter printers, these sticks are commonly produced in two differing shapes:

- The dominant shape east of the Rocky Mountains is the Elgin, or Eastern-pack shape. This shape was originally developed by the Elgin Butter Tub Company, founded in 1882 in Elgin, Illinois, and Rock Falls, Illinois. The sticks are 4¾ inches long and 1¼ inches (121 mm × 32 mm) wide, and are usually sold packed side-by-side in a rectangular container. Among the early butter printers to use this shape was the Elgin Butter Cutter.
- West of the Rocky Mountains, butter printers standardized on a different shape that is now referred to as the Western-pack shape. These butter sticks are 3¼ inches long and 1½ inches wide (80 mm × 38 mm) and are typically sold in cube-shaped boxes stacked two by two.

Both sticks contain the same amount of butter, although most butter dishes are designed for Elgin-style butter sticks.

The stick's wrapper is usually marked off as eight tablespoons (120 ml/4.2 imp fl oz; 4.1 US fl oz); the actual volume of one stick is approximately nine tablespoons (130 ml/4.6 imp fl oz; 4.4 US fl oz).

India produces and consumes more butter than any other nation, and allocates almost half of its annual milk pool to butter production. In 1997, India produced 1,470,000 metric tons (1,620,000 short tons) of butter, most of which was consumed domestically. Second in production was the United States (522,000 t/575,000 short tons), followed by France (466,000 t/514,000 short tons), Germany (442,000 t/487,000 short tons), and New Zealand (307,000 t/338,000 short tons). In terms of consumption, Germany was second after India, using 578,000 metric tons (637,000 short tons) of butter in 1997, followed by France (528,000 t/582,000 short tons), Russia (514,000 t/567,000 short tons), and the United States (505,000 t/557,000 short tons). New Zealand, Australia, and the Ukraine are among the few nations that export a significant percentage of the butter they produce.

Different varieties are found around the world. *Smen* is a spiced Moroccan clarified butter, buried in the ground and aged for months or years. Yak butter is important in Tibet; *tsampa*, barley flour mixed with yak butter, is a staple food. Butter tea is consumed in the Himalayan regions of Tibet, Bhutan, Nepal and India. It consists of tea served with intensely flavoured — or 'rancid' — yak butter and salt. In African and Asian developing nations, butter is traditionally made from sour milk rather than cream. It can take several hours of churning to produce workable butter grains from fermented milk.

## Storage and Cooking

Normal butter softens to a spreadable consistency around 15 °C (60 °F), well above refrigerator temperatures. The 'butter compartment' found in many refrigerators may be one of the warmer sections inside, but it still leaves butter quite hard. Until recently, many refrigerators sold in New Zealand featured a 'butter conditioner', a compartment kept warmer than the rest of the refrigerator—but still cooler than room temperature—with a small heater. Keeping butter tightly wrapped delays rancidity, which is hastened by exposure to light or air, and also helps prevent it from picking up other odors. Wrapped butter has a shelf life of several months at refrigerator temperatures.

'French butter dishes' or 'Acadian butter dishes' involve a lid with a long interior lip, which sits in a container holding a small amount of water. Usually the dish holds just enough water to submerge the interior lip when the dish is closed. Butter is packed into the lid. The water acts as a seal to keep the butter fresh, and also keeps the butter from overheating in hot temperatures. This allows butter to be safely stored on the countertop for several days without spoilage.

Once butter is softened, spices, herbs, or other flavouring agents can be mixed into it, producing what is called a *compound butter* or *composite butter* (sometimes also called *composed butter*). Compound butters can be used as spreads, or cooled, sliced, and placed onto hot food to melt into a sauce. Sweetened compound butters can be served with desserts; such hard sauces are often flavoured with spirits.

Melted butter plays an important role in the preparation of sauces, most obviously in French cuisine. *Beurre noisette* (hazel butter) and *Beurre noir* (black butter) are sauces of melted butter cooked until the milk solids and sugars have turned golden or dark brown; they are often finished with an addition of vinegar or lemon juice. Hollandaise and béarnaise sauces are emulsions of egg yolk and melted butter; they are in essence mayonnaises made with butter instead of oil. Hollandaise and béarnaise sauces are stabilized with the powerful emulsifiers in the egg yolks, but butter itself contains enough emulsifiers—mostly remnants of the fat globule membranes—to form a stable emulsion on its own. *Beurre blanc* (white butter) is made by whisking butter into reduced vinegar or wine, forming an emulsion with the texture of thick cream. *Beurre monté* (prepared butter) is melted but still emulsified butter; it lends its name to the practice of 'mounting' a sauce with butter: whisking cold butter into any water-based sauce at the end of cooking, giving the sauce a thicker body and a glossy shine—as well as a buttery taste.

In Poland, the butter lamb (*Baranek wielkanocny*) is a traditional addition to the Easter Meal for many Polish Catholics. Butter is shaped into a lamb either by hand or in a lamb-shaped mould.

Butter is used for sautéing and frying, although its milk solids brown and burn above 150°C (250°F)–a rather low temperature for most applications. The smoke point of butterfat is around 200°C (400°F), so clarified butter or ghee is better suited to frying. Ghee has always been a common frying medium in India, where many avoid other animal fats for cultural or religious reasons.

Butter fills several roles in baking, where it is used in a similar manner as other solid fats like lard, suet, or shortening, but has a flavour that may better complement sweet baked goods. Many cookie doughs and some cake batters are leavened, at least in part, by creaming butter and sugar together, which introduces air bubbles into the butter. The tiny bubbles locked within the butter expand in the heat of baking and aerate the cookie or cake. Some cookies like shortbread may have no other source of moisture but the water in the butter. Pastries like pie dough incorporate pieces of solid fat into the dough, which become flat layers of fat when the dough is rolled out. During baking, the fat melts away, leaving a flaky texture. Butter, because of its flavour, is a common choice for the fat in such a dough, but it can be more difficult to work with than shortening because of its low melting point. Pastry makers often chill all their ingredients and utensils while working with a butter dough.

According to USDA figures, one tablespoon of butter (14 grams/0.5 ounces) contains 420 kilojoules (100 kcal), all from fat, 11 grams (0.4 oz) of fat, of which 7 grams (0.25 oz) are saturated fat, and 30 milligrams (0.46 gr) of cholesterol. In other words, butter consists mostly of saturated fat and is a significant source of dietary cholesterol. For these reasons, butter has been generally considered to be a contributor to health problems, especially heart disease. For many years, vegetable margarine was recommended as a substitute, since it is an unsaturated fat and contains little or no cholesterol. In recent decades, though, it has become accepted that the trans fats contained in partially hydrogenated oils used in typical margarines significantly raise undesirable LDL cholesterol levels as well. Trans-fat free margarines have since been developed.

Proponents of the consumption of organic butter such as the nutritionist Mary Enig, state that since butter is nutritious and 'is rich in short and medium chain fatty acids', this can have a positive effect on health and prevent disease.

Butter contains only traces of lactose, so moderate consumption of butter is not a problem for the lactose intolerant. People with milk allergies need to avoid butter, which contains enough of the allergy-causing proteins to cause reactions.

Butter can form a useful role in dieting by providing satiety. A small amount added to low fat foods such as vegetables may stave off feelings of hunger.

# 8

# Casein

Casein (from Latin *caseus* 'cheese') is the predominant phosphoprotein (aS1, aS2, ß, ?) that accounts for nearly 80 per cent of proteins in cow milk and cheese. Milk-clotting proteases act on the soluble portion of the caseins, K-Casein, thus originating an unstable micellar state that results in clot formation. When coagulated with chymosin, casein is sometimes called paracasein. Chymosin (EC 3.4.23.4) is an aspartic protease that specifically hydrolyzes the peptide bond in Phe105-Met106 of ?-casein and is considered to be the most efficient protease for the cheese-making industry. British terminology, on the other hand, uses the term caseinogen for the uncoagulated protein and casein for the coagulated protein. As it exists in milk, it is a salt of calcium. Casein is not coagulated by heat. It is precipitated by acids and by rennet enzymes, a proteolytic enzyme typically obtained from the stomachs of calves. The enzyme trypsin can hydrolyze off a phosphate-containing peptone.

## Description

Casein consists of a fairly high number of proline peptides, which do not interact. There are also no disulfide bridges. As a result, it has relatively little tertiary structure. Because of this, it cannot denature. It is relatively hydrophobic, making it poorly soluble in water. It is found in milk as a suspension of particles called casein micelles which show some resemblance with surfactant-type micellae in a sense that the hydrophilic parts reside at the surface. The caseins in the micelles are held together by calcium ions and hydrophobic interactions. There are several models that account for the special conformation of casein in the micelles. One of them proposes that the micellar nucleus is formed by several submicelles, the periphery consisting of microvellosities of ?-casein. Another model suggests that the nucleus is formed by casein-interlinked fibrils. Finally, the most recent model proposes a double link among the caseins for gelling to take place. All 3 models consider micelles as colloidal particles formed by casein aggregates wrapped up in soluble ?-casein molecules.

The isoelectric point of casein is 4.6. Since milk's pH is 6.6, casein has a negative charge in milk. The purified protein is water insoluble. While it is also insoluble in neutral salt solutions, it is readily dispersible in dilute alkalis and in salt solutions such as sodium oxalate and sodium acetate.

Casein has been reported to reduce tooth decay.

## Protein Supplement

### *Slow Acting*

An attractive property of the casein molecule is its ability to form a gel or clot in the stomach. The ability to form this clot makes it very efficient in nutrient supply. The clot is able to provide a sustained slow release of amino acids into the blood stream, sometimes lasting for several hours. This provides better nitrogen retention and utilization by the body.

### IGF-1

Plasma immunoreactive IGF-1 concentration in rats given a casein diet was higher than that in rats given a soya-bean-protein or protein-free diet.

Casein has been documented to break down to produce the peptide casomorphin, an opioid that appears to act primarily as a histamine releaser. Some believe that this casomorphine aggravates the symptoms of autism. A 2006 review of seven studies indicated that although benefits were seen in all studies from the introduction of elimination diets (e.g., casein or gluten free) in the treatment of autism spectrum disorders, none of the studies were performed in a manner to create an unbiased scientific opinion. Preliminary data from the first and only double-blind randomized control trial of a gluten and casein-free diet "indicated no statistically significant findings even though several parents reported improvement in their children." Research has shown of high rates of use of complementary and alternative therapies (CAM) for children with autism including gluten and/or casein exclusion diets. Evidence for efficacy of these diets is currently unsubstantiated.

Four casein proteins make up about 80 per cent of the protein in cow's milk. One of the major caseins is beta-casein, of which there are several types, but 'A1' and 'A2' are the most common. Certain breeds of cows, such as Frisians, the main breed in Europe, produce A2 milk which is A1 free, alongside other breeds, such as Guernseys, as well as sheep and goats, which also produce mostly A2 milk.

In 1993 Professor Bob Elliott from Auckland University, looking into the incidence of Type 1 diabetes amongst Samoan children started investigating potential links with milk and the proportion of A1 to A2 beta-casein proteins — which varies considerably between the herds in different countries. One of the scientist involved, Dr Corann McLachlan, teamed up with entrepreneur Howard Patterson to form A2 Corporation, licensing technology to quickly test the DNA of cattle to see which type they produce, a their 'A2 milk' trademark.

### Casein-free Diet

Casein has a molecular structure that is quite similar to that of gluten. Thus, some gluten-free diets are combined with casein-free diets and referred to as a gluten-free, casein-free diet. Casein is often listed as sodium caseinate, calcium caseinate or milk protein. These are often found in energy bars, drinks, and packaged goods.

## Altering the Effects of Polyphenols

A study of Charité Hospital in Berlin by Lorenzo et al., published in The European Heart Journal, showed that adding milk to tea causes the casein to bind to the molecules in tea that cause the arteries to relax, especially a catechin molecule called EGCG. A similar study by Reddy et al. (2005) suggests that the addition of milk to tea does not alter the antioxidant activity in vivo and the cardiovascular effect remains controversial. A study published in the journal Free Radical Biology and Medicine indicates that casein reduced the peak plasma levels of beneficial polyphenols after the consumption of blueberries.

## Lactation

Lactation describes the secretion of milk from the mammary glands, the process of providing that milk to the young, and the period of time that a mother lactates to feed her young. The process occurs in all female mammals, and in humans it is commonly referred to as breastfeeding or nursing. In most species milk comes out of the mother's nipples; however, the platypus (a non-placental mammal) releases milk through ducts in its abdomen. In only one species of mammal, the Dayak fruit bat, is milk production a normal male function. In some other mammals, the male may produce milk as the result of a hormone imbalance. This phenomenon may also be observed in newborn infants as well (for instance witch's milk).

*Galactopoiesis* is the maintenance of milk production. This stage requires prolactin (PRL) and oxytocin.

From the fourth month of pregnancy (the second and third trimesters), a woman's body produces hormones that stimulate the growth of the milk duct system in the breasts:

- ❖ ***Progesterone*** — influences the growth in size of alveoli and lobes. Progesterone levels drop after birth. This triggers the onset of copious milk production.
- ❖ ***Oestrogen*** — stimulates the milk duct system to grow and become specific. Oestrogen levels also drop at delivery and remain low for the first several months of breastfeeding. It is recommended that breastfeeding mothers avoid oestrogen-based birth control methods, as a spike in estrogen levels may reduce a mother's milk supply.

Follicle stimulating hormone (FSH)

Luteinizing hormone (LH)

- ❖ ***Prolactin*** — contributes to the increased growth of the alveoli during pregnancy.
- ❖ ***Oxytocin*** — contracts the smooth muscle of the uterus during and after birth, and during orgasm(s). After birth, oxytocin contracts the smooth muscle layer of band-like cells surrounding the alveoli to squeeze the newly-produced milk into the duct system. Oxytocin is necessary for the *milk ejection reflex*, or *let-down* to occur.

***Human placental lactogen* (*HPL*)** — From the second month of pregnancy, the placenta releases large amounts of HPL. This hormone appears to be instrumental in breast, nipple, and areola growth before birth.

By the fifth or sixth month of pregnancy, the breasts are ready to produce milk. It is also possible to induce lactation without pregnancy.

During the latter part of pregnancy, the woman's breasts enter into the *Lactogenesis I* stage. This is when the breasts make colostrum, a thick, sometimes yellowish fluid. At this stage, high levels of progesterone inhibit most milk production. It is not a medical concern if a pregnant woman leaks any colostrum before her baby's birth, nor is it an indication of future milk production.

**Lactogenesis II**

At birth, prolactin levels remain high, while the delivery of the placenta results in a sudden drop in progesterone, estrogen, and HPL levels. This abrupt withdrawal of progesterone in the presence of high prolactin levels stimulates the copious milk production of *Lactogenesis II*.

When the breast is stimulated, prolactin levels in the blood rise, peak in about 45 minutes, and return to the pre-breastfeeding state about three hours later. The release of prolactin triggers the cells in the alveoli to make milk. Prolactin also transfers to the breast milk. Some research indicates that prolactin in milk is higher at times of higher milk production, and lower when breasts are fuller, and that the highest levels tend to occur between 2 a.m. and 6 a.m.

***Other hormones*** — notably insulin, thyroxine, and cortisol – are also involved, but their roles are not yet well understood. Although biochemical markers indicate that Lactogenesis II begins about 30-40 hours after birth, mothers do not typically begin feeling increased breast fullness (the sensation of milk 'coming in the breast') until 50-73 hours (2-3 days) after birth.

Colostrum is the first milk a breastfed baby receives. It contains higher amounts of white blood cells and antibodies than mature milk, and is especially high in immunoglobulin A (IgA), which coats the lining of the baby's immature intestines, and helps to prevent germs from invading the baby's system. Secretory IgA also helps prevent food allergies. Over the first two weeks after the birth, colostrum production slowly gives way to mature breast milk.

**Lactogenesis III**

The hormonal endocrine control system drives milk production during pregnancy and the first few days after the birth. When the milk supply is more firmly established, autocrine (or local) control system begins. This stage is called *Lactogenesis III.*

During this stage, the more that milk is removed from the breasts, the more the breast will produce milk. Research also suggests that draining the breasts more fully also increases the rate of milk production. Thus the milk supply is strongly influenced by how often the baby feeds and how well it is able to transfer milk from the breast. Low supply can often be traced to:

- not feeding or pumping often enough

Inability of the infant to transfer milk effectively caused by, among other things:

- jaw or mouth structure deficits;
- poor latching technique;
- rare maternal endocrine disorders;
- hypoplastic breast tissue;
- a metabolic or digestive inability in the infant, making it unable to digest the milk it receives;
- inadequate calorie intake or malnutrition of the mother.

## Milk Ejection Reflex

The release of the hormone oxytocin leads to the *milk ejection* or *let-down reflex*. Oxytocin stimulates the muscles surrounding the breast to squeeze out the milk. Breastfeeding mothers describe the sensation differently. Some feel a slight tingling, others feel immense amounts of pressure or slight pain/discomfort, and still others do not feel anything different.

The let-down reflex is not always consistent, especially at first. The thought of breastfeeding or the sound of any baby can stimulate this reflex, causing unwanted leakage, or both breasts may give out milk when an infant is feeding from one breast. However, this and other problems often settle after two weeks of feeding. Stress or anxiety can cause difficulties with breastfeeding.

A poor milk ejection reflex can be due to sore or cracked nipples, separation from the infant, a history of breast surgery, or tissue damage from prior breast trauma. If a mother has trouble breastfeeding, different methods of assisting the milk ejection reflex may help. These include feeding in a familiar and comfortable location, massage of the breast or back, or warming the breast with a cloth or shower.

**Afterpains**

The surge of oxytocin that may also possibly trigger the milk ejection reflex also causes the uterus to contract. During breastfeeding, mothers may feel these contractions as *afterpains*. These may range from period-like cramps to strong labour-like contractions and can be more severe with second and subsequent babies. Some women's breasts also become dry and chapped and even crack open and bleed while breast feeding. Rubbing lanolin on the nipples and areola can help with those problems, as can using Vaseline.

Milk production can be 'artificially' and intentionally obtained in the absence of pregnancy in the woman. It is not necessary that the woman has ever been pregnant, and she can be well in her post-menopausal period. Women who have never been pregnant are sometimes able to induce enough lactation to breastfeed. This is called 'induced lactation'. Women who have breastfed before can re-start. This is called 'relactation'. This is how some adoptive mothers, usually beginning with a supplemental nursing system or some other form of supplementation, can breastfeed. There is thought to be little or no difference in milk composition whether lactation is artificially induced or a result of pregnancy.

Lactation can be induced by physical stimulation and by drugs. In principle — with considerable patience and perseverance — it is possible to induce lactation by sucking on the nipples alone. The nipples may need to be consistently stimulated by a breast pump or actual suckling (several times a day), and the breasts massaged and squeezed ("milked") to encourage flow of any milk. Temporary use of galactagogue (milk-inducing) drugs is also effective; galactagogue herbs may also be of use. Once established, lactation responds to demand.

## Raw Milk

Raw milk is milk that has not been pasteurized or homogenized.

Humans consumed raw milk exclusively prior to the industrial revolution and the discovery of the pasteurization process in 1864. During the industrial revolution large populations congregated into urban areas detached from the agricultural lifestyle. Up until that point, individuals and families owned their own goats, cows, and other livestock and milked them on a daily basis.

Pasteurization was first used in the United States in the 1890s after the discovery of germ theory to control the hazards of highly contagious bacterial diseases including bovine tuberculosis and brucellosis that was thought to be easily transmitted to humans through the drinking of raw milk. Initially after the scientific discovery of bacteria, no product testing was available to determine if a farmer's milk was safe or infected, so all milk was treated as potentially contagious. After the first test was developed, some farmers actively worked to prevent their infected animals from being killed and removed from food production, or would falsify the test results so that their animals would appear to be free of infection.

When it was first used, pasteurization was thought to make raw milk from any source safer to consume. More recently, farm sanitation has greatly improved and effective testing has been developed for bovine tuberculosis and other diseases, making other approaches to ensuring safety of milk more feasible; however pasteurization continues to be widely used in case infectious milk should enter the food supply.

### The Raw *vs.* Pasteurized Debate

The *Raw* vs. *Pasteurized Debate* places the alleged health benefits of consuming raw milk against the disease threat of unpasteurized milk. Although agencies such as the Centers for Disease Control (CDC), the Food and Drug Administration (FDA), and other worldwide regulatory agencies say that pathogens from raw milk make it unsafe to consume, other organizations such as the Weston A. Price Foundation in its 'Real Milk' campaign say that raw milk has health benefits that are destroyed in the pasteurization process and that it can be produced hygienically.

The disease threat at present is a statistical issue and is defined in public health terms. Although *Mycobacteria bovis* (non-pulmonary tuberculosis) is found in raw milk, it is relatively rare in modern industrial societies. The public health issue is that tuberculosis and typhoid will always be present in raw milk, even if in statistically small amounts. These potentially disastrous pathogens in raw milk (non-pulmonary tuberculosis, typhoid, and salmonella) can be safely controlled by pasteurization, animal husbandry, and proper milk storage methods. The health of dairy animals can be managed by continual testing of dairy herds and careful storage of milk products. Some pathogens can not be eliminated from dairy herds since the pathogens are carried by common wildlife (goats, cats, dogs, pigs, buffalo, badgers, possums, deer, and bison) . Thus, the public health side of the debate always returns to *pasteurization*.

In 2007 Kansas State University published a list of outbreaks associated with consuming raw milk or dairy products and an article about the investigation of raw milk outbreaks.

In 2008 scientists noticed that raw milk contains more bacteria than previously thought and identified Chryseobacterium oranimense as well as C. haifense and C. bovis, but the amount found in raw milk has not been proven harmful.

## Legal Status

### *Worldwide*

Regulation of the commercial distribution of packaged raw milk varies across the world. Some countries have complete bans, but many have partial bans that do not restrict the purchase of raw milk bought directly from the farmer. Raw milk is sometimes distributed through a cow share programme, wherein the consumer owns a share in the dairy animal or the herd, and can be considered to be consuming milk from their own animal. Raw milk is sometimes marketed for animal or pet consumption, or for other uses such as soap making in places where sales for human consumption are prohibited.

### In Africa

Although milk consumption in Africa is fairly low compared to the rest of the world, in tribes where milk consumption is popular, such as the Maasai tribe, milk is typically consumed unpasteurized.

### In Europe

Milk is typically consumed unpasteurized in rural areas of Europe, and raw milk can typically be found in small amounts at stores in large cities. Raw milk cheese is legally produced in most European countries.

Distribution of raw milk is illegal in Scotland. While it is legal in England, Wales, and Northern Ireland, the only registered producers are in England. About 200 producers sell raw, or 'green top' milk direct to consumers, either at the farm, at a Farmers' market, or through a delivery service.

The bottle must display the warning 'this product has not been heat-treated and may contain organisms harmful to health', and the dairy must conform to higher hygiene standards than dairies producing only pasteurised milk.

**In Asia**

In rural areas of Asia where milk consumption is popular, milk is typically unpasteurized. In large cities of Asia, raw milk, especially from water buffalo, is typical. In most countries of Asia, laws prohibiting raw milk are nonexistent or rarely enforced.

**In Australia**

Raw milk for drinking purposes is illegal in all states and territories in Australia, as is all raw cheese. This has been circumvented somewhat by selling raw milk as *bath milk*. An exception to the cheese rule has been made recently for two Roquefort cheeses. There is some indication of share owning cows, allowing the 'owners' to consume the raw milk, but also evidence that the government is trying to close this loophole.

**In Canada**

'No person shall sell the normal lacteal secretion obtained from the mammary gland of the cow, genus Bos, or of any other animal, or sell a dairy product made with any such secretion, unless the secretion or dairy product has been pasteurized by being held at a temperature and for a period that ensure the reduction of the alkaline phosphatase activity so as to meet the tolerances specified in official method MFO-3, Determination of Phosphatase Activity in Dairy Products, dated November 30, 1981'.

However, Canada permits the sale of raw milk cheeses that are aged over 60 days. In 2009, the province of Quebec modified regulations to allow raw milk cheeses aged less than 60 days provided stringent safeguards are met.

### In the United States

Twenty-eight U.S. states do not prohibit sales of raw milk. Cow shares can be found, and raw milk purchased for animal consumption in many states where retail for human consumption is prohibited.

Most states impose restrictions on raw milk suppliers due to concerns about safety. As of 2009, the state of Connecticut has discussed creating possible restrictions upon the sale of raw milk to farms and farmer's markets. The FDA reports that, in 2002, consuming partially heated raw milk and raw milk products caused 200 Americans to become ill in some manner.

Many governmental officials hold to the need for pasteurization. Before pasteurization, many dairies, especially in cities, fed their cattle on low-quality food, and their milk was rife with dangerous bacteria. Pasteurizing it was the only way to make it safely drinkable. As pasteurization has been standard for many years, it is now widely assumed that raw milk is dangerous.

Proponents of raw milk (in the US) advance two basic arguments for unpasteurized milk. They claim that pasteurization destroys or damages some of the milk's nutrients, and that while pasteurization may kill dangerous bacteria, it also kills off 'good' bacteria that raw milk supporters claim to have health benefits. The United States Food and Drug administration claims that this is false, and that pasteurizing milk does not destroy any of its nutritive value.

9

# Condensed Milk

Condensed milk, also known as sweetened condensed milk, is cow's milk from which water has been removed and to which sugar has been added, yielding a very thick, sweet product which when canned can last for years without refrigeration if unopened. The two terms, condensed milk and sweetened condensed milk, have become synonymous; though there have been unsweetened condensed milk products, today these are uncommon. Condensed milk is used in numerous dessert dishes in many countries, especially in Russia and the former Soviet Union where it is known as '(*sguschyonka*, literally' [that which is] thickened").

A related product is evapourated milk, which has undergone a more complex process and which is not sweetened.

According to the writings of Marco Polo, the Tartars were able to condense milk. Ten pounds (4.54 kg) of milk paste was carried by each man who would mix the product with water. However, this probably refers to the soft Tartar curd which can be made into a drink ('ayran') by diluting it, and therefore refers to fermented, not fresh, milk concentrate.

Nicolas Appert condensed milk in France in 1820, and Gail Borden, Jr. in the United States in 1856 in reaction to difficulties in storing milk for more than a few hours. Before this development milk could only be kept fresh for a short while and was only available in the immediate vicinity of a cow. While returning from a trip to England in 1851, Borden was devastated by the death of several children, apparently due to poor milk from shipboard cows. With less than a year of schooling and following in a wake of failures, both of his own and of others, Borden was inspired by the vacuum pan he had seen being used by Shakers to condense fruit juice and was at last able to reduce milk without scorching or curdling it. Even then his first two factories failed and only the third, built with his new partner, Jeremiah Milbank in Wassaic, New York, produced a usable milk derivative that was long-lasting and needed no refrigeration.

Probably of equal importance for the future of milk were Borden's requirements (the 'Dairyman's Ten Commandments') for farmers who wanted to sell him raw milk: they were required to wash udders before milking, keep barns swept clean, and scald and dry their strainers morning and night. By 1858 Borden's milk, sold as Eagle Brand, had gained a reputation for purity, durability and economy.

In 1864, Gail Borden's New York Condensed Milk Company constructed the New York Milk Condensery in Brewster, New York. This condensery was the largest and most advanced milk factory and was Borden's first commercially successful plant. Over 200 dairy farmers supplied 20,000 gallons (76,000 litres) of milk daily to the Brewster plant as demand was driven by the Civil War.

The U.S. government ordered huge amounts of it as a field ration for Union soldiers during the American Civil War. This was an extraordinary field ration for the nineteenth century: a typical 14 oz (400 g) can contains 1,300 calories (5440 kJ), 1 oz (30 g) each of protein and fat, and more than 7 oz (200 g) of carbohydrate.

Soldiers returning home from the Civil War soon spread the word. By the late 1860s, condensed milk was a major product. The first Canadian condensery was built at Truro, Nova Scotia, in 1871. In 1899, E. B. Stuart opened the first Pacific Coast Condensed Milk Company (later known as the Carnation Milk Products Company) plant in Kent, Washington. Unfortunately, the condensed milk market developed a bubble. Too many manufacturers chased too little demand. By 1912, stocks of condensed milk were large and the price dropped. Many condenseries went out of business. In 1911, Nestlé constructed the world's largest condensed milk plant in Dennington, Victoria, Australia.

In 1914, Professor Otto F Hunziker, head of Purdue University's dairy department, self-published *Condensed milk and milk powder: prepared for the use of milk condenseries, dairy students and pure food departments*. This text, along with additional work of Professor Hunziker and others involved with the American Dairy Science Association, standardized and improved condensery operations in the U.S. and internationally. Hunziker's book was republished in a seventh edition in October 2007 by Cartwright Press.

The first World War regenerated interest in, and a market for, condensed milk, primarily due to its storage and transportation benefits. In the U.S., the higher price for raw milk paid by condenseries created significant problems for the cheese industry.

**Production**

Raw milk is clarified and standardized, and then is heated to 85-90ºC for several seconds. This heating destroys some microorganisms, decreases fat separation and inhibits oxidation. Some water is evaporated from the milk and sugar is added to approximately 45 per cent. This sugar is what extends the shelf life of sweetened condensed milk. Sucrose increases the liquid's osmotic pressure, which prevents microorganism growth. The sweetened evaporated milk is cooled and lactose crystallization is induced.

## Current Use

Condensed milk is used in recipes for the popular Brazilian candy brigadeiro in which condensed milk is the main ingredient (the most famous condensed milk brand in Brazil is Moça ['mo.s?], local version of Swiss *Milch Mädchen* marketed by Nestlé), lemon meringue pie, key lime pie, caramel candies and other desserts.

In parts of Asia and Europe, sweetened condensed milk is the preferred milk to be added to coffee or sweetened tea. Many countries in South East Asia use condensed milk to flavour their coffee. A popular treat in Asia is to put condensed milk on toast and eat it in a similar way as jam and toast. Nestlé has even produced a squeeze bottle similar to Smucker's jam squeeze bottles for this very purpose. Condensed milk is a major ingredient in many Indian desserts and sweets. While most Indians start with normal milk to reduce and sweeten it, packaged condensed milk has also become popular.

In New Orleans, it is commonly used as a topping on top of a chocolate or similar cream flavor snowball. In Scotland, it is mixed with sugar and some butter and baked to form a popular, sweet candy called Tablet (confectionery) or Swiss-Milk-Tablet. In some parts of the Southern U.S., condensed milk is a key ingredient in lemon icebox pie, a sort of cream pie. In the Philippines, condensed milk is mixed with some evaporated milk and eggs, spooned into shallow metal containers over liquid caramelised sugar, then steamed to make a stiffer and more filling version of crème brulée known as leche flan.

During the communism era in Poland it was common to boil a can of condensed milk in water for about 2 hours. The resulting product is called kaymak - sweet semiliquid substance which can be used as a cake icing or put between dry wafers. It is less common nowadays but recently some manufactures of condensed milk introduced canned readymade kaymak. Boiling the can in this way is central to the making of Banoffee pie and home-made dulce de leche.

**Evaporated Milk**

Evaporated milk, also known as dehydrated milk, is a shelf-stable canned milk product with about 60 per cent of the water removed from fresh milk. It differs from sweetened condensed milk, which contains added sugar. Sweetened condensed milk requires less processing since the added sugar inhibits bacterial growth.

The actual liquid portion of the product takes up half the space of fresh milk. When the non-liquid product is mixed with a proportionate amount of water, evaporated milk becomes the equivalent of fresh milk. This makes evaporated milk attractive for shipping purposes and can have a shelf life of months or even years, depending upon the brand. This made evaporated milk very popular before refrigeration as a safe and reliable substitute for perishable fresh milk, that could be shipped easily to locations lacking the means of safe milk production or storage. Households in the western world use it most often today for desserts and baking due to its unique flavour. It is also used as a substitute for pouring cream, as an accompaniment to desserts, or (undiluted) as a rich substitute for milk.

Evaporated milk was invented in the 1880s, after John B. Meyenberg emigrated to the U.S. from Switzerland where he had devised the process, but had no support to begin production. He obtained two U.S. patents for his process and sterilizing apparatus, issued on November 25, 1884. He formed the Helvetia Milk Condensing Company on February 14, 1885, with a number of farmers and businessmen of Highland, Illinois, as stockholders. By June 14, 1885, the first canned 'Highland Evaporated Cream' was ready to be marketed.

The process involved the evaporation of about half the water from the milk, after which the product was homogenized, canned and sterilized.

There were problems with the new product, with premature spoilage in early batches. Over the next few years, Louis Latzer and Dr. Werner Schmidt solved the problems which had been found to be caused by bacteria. With the marketing efforts of John Wilde, the company became successful as Pet, Inc., and is now part of The J.M. Smucker Co.

John P. Meyenberg, son of John B. Meyenberg, was the first American to evaporate goat's milk. He started the Meyenberg business in 1934, supplying goat milk products that are more digestible than cow's milk, and an alternative for people (like himself) who were allergic to cow's milk.

## Evaporated Milk Formulas

In the 1920s and 1930s, evaporated milk began to be widely commercially available at low prices, and several clinical studies suggested that babies fed evaporated milk formula thrive as well as breastfed babies. These findings are not supported by modern research.

## Definition

Evaporated milk is fresh, homogenized milk from which 60 per cent of the water has been removed. After the water has been removed, the product is chilled, stabilized, packaged and sterilized. A slightly caramelized flavor results from the high heat process, and it is slightly darker in colour than fresh milk. The evaporation process also concentrates the nutrients and the food energy. Thus, for the same weight, undiluted evaporated milk contains more food energy than fresh milk.

According to the United States Code of Federal Regulations (Title 21, Chapter 1, Part 131, Sub part B, Section 130) evaporated milk:

(a) ***Description*** — Evaporated milk is the liquid food obtained by partial removal of water only from milk. It contains not less than 6.5 per cent by weight of milk fat, not less than 16.5 per cent by weight of milk solids not fat, and not less than 23 per cent by weight of total milk solids. Evaporated milk contains added vitamin D as prescribed by paragraph (b) of this section. It is homogenized. It is sealed in a container and so processed by heat, either before or after sealing, as to prevent spoilage.

Sections (b)-(f) of the above code regulate vitamin addition, optional ingredients, methods of analysis, nomenclature, and label declaration.

### In Malaysia

In Malaysia, due to price controls, evaporated (and condensed) milk contains palm oil. It is one of the ingredients to make *Teh Tarik* in Malaysia and Singapore. Also it is added in brewed tea and coffee to make *Teh See* and *Kopi C* respectively.

### Powdered Milk

Powdered Milk is a manufactured dairy product made by evapourating milk to dryness. One purpose of drying milk is to preserve it; milk powder has a far longer shelf life than liquid milk and does not need to be refrigerated, due to its low moisture content. Another purpose is to reduce its bulk for economy of transportation. Powdered milk and dairy products include such items as dry whole milk, non-fat dry milk, dry buttermilk, dry whey products and dry dairy blends.

While Marco Polo wrote of Mongolian Tatar troops in the time of Kublai Khan carrying sun-dried skimmed milk as 'a kind of paste', the first usable commercial production of dried milk was invented by the Russian chemist M. Dirchoff in 1832. In 1855, T.S. Grimwade took a patent on a dried milk procedure, though a William Newton had patented a vacuum drying process as early as 1837. Today, powdered milk is usually made by spray drying non-fat skim milk, whole milk, buttermilk or whey. Pasteurized milk is first concentrated in an evaporator to about 50 per cent milk solids. The resulting concentrated milk is sprayed into a heated chamber where the water almost instantly evaporates, leaving fine particles of powdered milk solids.

Alternatively, the milk can be dried by drum drying. Milk is applied as a thin film to the surface of a heated drum, and the dried milk solids are then scraped off. Powdered milk made this way tends to have a cooked flavour, due to caramelization caused by greater heat exposure.

Another process is freeze drying, which preserves many nutrients in milk, compared to drum drying.

The drying method and the heat treatment of the milk as it is processed alters the properties of the milk powder (for example, solubility in cold water, flavour, bulk density).

**Uses**

Powdered milk is frequently used in the manufacture of infant formula, confectionery such as chocolate and caramel candy, and in recipes for baked goods where adding liquid milk would render the product too thin. Powdered milk is also widely used in various sweets such as the famous Indian milk balls known as Rasa-Gulla and popular Indian sweet delicacy (sprinkled with desiccated coconut) known as Chum chum (made with skim milk powder).

Powdered milk is also a common item in UN food aid supplies, fallout shelters, warehouses, and wherever fresh milk is not a viable option. It is widely used in many developing countries because of reduced transport and storage costs (reduced bulk and weight, no refrigerated vehicles). As with other dry foods, it is considered nonperishable, and is favored by survivalists, hikers, and others requiring nonperishable, easy-to-prepare food.

Reconstituting one cup of milk from powdered milk requires one cup of potable water and one-third cup of powdered milk.

Powdered milk is also used in western blots as a blocking buffer to prevent nonspecific protein interactions , and is referred to as Blotto.

Commercial milk powders are reported to contain oxysterols (oxidized cholesterol) in higher amounts than in fresh milk (up to 30µg/g, versus trace amounts in fresh milk). The oxysterol free radicals have been suspected of being initiators of atherosclerotic plaques . For comparison, powdered eggs contain even more oxysterols, up to 200µg/g.

## Market

Fonterra, a New Zealand based multinational company, is the world's largest producer of milk powder controlling 40 per cent of the global whole milkpowder. The dominance of New Zealand in the global dairy industry, for example Fonterra controls around 30 per cent of the world's dairy exports has prompted the formation of a futures market for trading whole milkpowder.

## Adulteration

In the 2008 Chinese milk scandal, melamine adulterant was found in Sanlu infant formula, added to fool tests into reporting higher protein content. Thousands became ill and some children died after consuming the product.

## Food and Health

### *Nutritional Value*

Milk powders contain all twenty standard amino acids (the building blocks of proteins) and are high in soluble vitamins and minerals. According to USAID the typical average amounts of major nutrients in the unreconstituted milk are (by weight) 36 per cent protein, 52 per cent carbohydrates (predominantly lactose), calcium 1.3 per cent, potassium 1.8 per cent. Their milk powder is fortified with Vitamin A and D, 3000IU and 600IU respectively per 100g. Inappropriate storage conditions (high relative humidity and high ambient temperature) can significantly degrade the nutritive value of milk powder.

## Cream Cheese

Cream cheese (also called soft cheese) is a sweet, soft, mild-tasting, white cheese, defined by the US Department of Agriculture as containing at least 33 per cent milkfat (as marketed) with a moisture content of not more than 55 per cent, and a pH range of 4.4 to 4.9.

Cream cheese is not naturally matured and is meant to be consumed fresh, and so it differs from other soft cheeses such as Brie and Neufchâtel. More comparable in taste, texture, and production methods are Boursin and Mascarpone.

There are French references to cream cheese as early as 1651. References to cream cheese in England start from at least 1754 and recipes follow soon after, particularly from Lincolnshire and the southwest of England.

According to the American food processing company Kraft Foods, the first American cream cheese was made in New York in 1872 by American dairyman William Lawrence. In 1880, 'Philadelphia' was adopted as the brand name, after the city that was considered at the time to be the home of top quality food.

The technique is known to have been in use in Normandy since the 1850s, producing cheeses with higher fat content than the US model, and *Philadelphia* cream cheese has been suggested as a substitute when *petit suisse* is not available.

*Philadelphia* is used by some as a generic term for cream cheese, and in Spanish it is translated as *queso Filadelfia* or 'queso crema'.

Cream cheese is typically used in savoury snacks of various types (for example, as a spread on bread, bagels, crackers, various types of raw vegetables, etc.), and can be used in cheesecakes and salads. It can also be used to make cheese sauces. It can be a base to some spreads, such as yogurt-cream cheese topping for graham crackers, (10 oz cream cheese, and 1 cup yogurt, whipped). It is sometimes used in place of butter (or alongside butter in a ratio of two parts cream cheese to one part butter) when making cakes or cookies, and it is also used to make cream cheese icing, which is similar to buttercream icing, (using a ratio of two parts cream cheese to one part butter) which is used to ice carrot cake. It is the main ingredient in crab rangoon, an appetizer commonly served at American Chinese restaurants. It can also be used instead of butter or olive oil in mashed potatoes to create a creamy taste.

Cream cheese is difficult to manufacture. Normally, protein molecules in milk have a negative surface charge, which keeps milk in a liquid state; the molecules act as surfactants, forming micelles around the particles of fat and keeping it in emulsion. Lactic acid bacteria are added to pasteurized and homogenized milk. During the fermentation at around 23°C, the pH level of the milk decreases. Amino acids at the surface of the proteins begin losing charge and become neutral, turning the fat micelles from hydrophilic to hydrophobic state and causing the liquid to coagulate. If the bacteria are left in the milk too long, the pH lowers further, the micelles attain a positive charge and the mixture returns to liquid form. The key then is to kill the bacteria by heating the mixture to 52-63°C at the moment the cheese is in an isoelectric point, meaning the state at which half the ionizable surface amino acids of the proteins are positively charged and half are negative. Inaccurate timing of heating leads to an inferior or unusable product.

However, subtle changes in the timing of the process can result in variations in flavor and texture. Furthermore, because cream cheese has a higher fat content than other cheeses, and fat repels water, which tends to separate from the cheese, stabilizers such as guar and carob gums are added to prolong its shelf life.

Improper heat treatment of milk may lead to formation of hard particles of amorphous compacted protein, causing unpleasant grittiness.

10

# Yoghurt

Yoghurt or yogurt is a dairy product produced by bacterial fermentation of milk. Fermentation of lactose produces lactic acid, which acts on milk protein to give yoghurt its texture and its characteristic tang. Soy yoghurt, a non-dairy yoghurt alternative, is made from soy milk. Dairy yoghurt is produced using a culture of *Lactobacillus delbrueckii* subsp. *bulgaricus* and *Streptococcus salivarius* subsp. *thermophilus* bacteria. Milk is heated and cooled for an hour. While it is heated, the bacteria are added for fermentation.

People have been making — and eating — yogurt for at least 5,400 years. Today it is a common food item throughout the world. A nutritious food with unique health benefits, it is rich in protein, calcium, riboflavin, vitamin B6 and vitamin B12.

The word is derived from Turkish *yogurt*, and is related to *yogurmak* 'to knead' and *yogun* 'dense' or 'thick'. The letter g was traditionally rendered as 'gh' in transliterations of Turkish, which used to be written in a variant of the Arabic alphabet until the introduction of the Latin alphabet in 1928. In older Turkish the letter denoted a voiced velar fricative but this sound is elided between back vowels in modern Turkish, in which the word is pronounced. Some eastern dialects retain the consonant in this position, and Turks in the Balkans pronounce the word with a hard /g/.

In English, there are several variations of the spelling of the word; in Australia and New Zealand 'yoghurt' prevails. In the United Kingdom 'yoghurt' and 'yogurt' are both current, 'yoghurt' being more common, and 'yoghourt' is an uncommon alternative. In the United States, 'yogurt' is the usual spelling and 'yoghurt' a minor variant. In Canada, Canadian brands typically use 'yogourt' as it is correct in both official languages, however 'yogurt' is used as well and is common among English speakers.

Whatever the spelling, the word is usually pronounced with a short *o* in the UK, with a long *o* in North America, Australia and South Africa, and with either a long or short *o* in New Zealand and Ireland.

There is evidence of cultured milk products being produced as food for at least 4,500 years. The earliest yoghurts were probably spontaneously fermented by wild bacteria *Lactobacillus delbrueckii subsp. bulgaricus* native to and named after Bulgaria.

The oldest writings mentioning yogurt are attributed to Pliny the Elder who remarked that certain nomadic tribes, including the Bulgars, knew how "to thicken the milk into a substance with an agreeable acidity". The use of yoghurt by medieval Turks is recorded in the books *Diwan Lughat al-Turk* by Mahmud Kashgari and *Kutadgu Bilig* by Yusuf Has Hajib written in the 11th century. Both texts mention the word 'yoghurt' in different sections and describe its use by nomadic Turks. An early account of a European encounter with yoghurt occurs in French clinical history: Francis I suffered from a severe diarrhea which no French doctor could cure. His ally Suleiman the Magnificent sent a doctor, who allegedly cured the patient with yoghurt. Being grateful, the French king spread around the information about the food which had cured him.

Until the 1900s, yoghurt was a staple in diets of people in the Russian Empire (and especially Central Asia and the Caucasus), Western Asia, South Eastern Europe/Balkans, Central Europe, and India. Bulgarian student of medicine in Geneva Stamen Grigorov (1878-1945) first examined the microflora of the Bulgarian yoghurt. In 1905 he described it as consisting of a spherical and a rod-like lactic acid bacteria. In 1907 the rod-like bacteria was called *Lactobacillus bulgaricus* (now *Lactobacillus delbrueckii subsp. bulgaricus*). The Russian Nobel laureat biologist Ilya Ilyich Mechnikov, from the Institut Pasteur in Paris, was influenced by Grigorov's work and hypothesised that regular consumption of yoghurt was responsible for the unusually long lifespans of Bulgarian peasants. Believing *Lactobacillus* to be essential for good health, Mechnikov worked to popularise yoghurt as a foodstuff throughout Europe.

A Sephardic Jewish entrepreneur named Isaac Carasso industrialized the production of yoghurt. In 1919, Carasso, who was from Ottoman Salonika, started a small yoghurt business in Barcelona and named the business Danone ('little Daniel') after his son. The brand later expanded to the United States under an Americanised version of the name: *Dannon*.

Yoghurt with added fruit jam was patented in 1933 by the Radlická Mlékárna dairy in Prague. It was introduced to the United States in 1947, by Dannon.

Yoghurt was first introduced to the United States by Armenian immigrants Sarkis and Rose Colombosian, who started 'Colombo and Sons Creamery' in Andover, Massachusetts in 1929. Colombo Yogurt was originally delivered around New England in a horse-drawn wagon inscribed with the Armenian word 'madzoon' which was later changed to 'yogurt', the Turkish name of the product, as Turkish was the lingua franca between immigrants of the various Near Eastern ethnicities who were the main consumers at that time. Yoghurt's popularity in the United States was enhanced in the 1950s and 1960s when it was presented as a health food. By the late 20th century yoghurt had become a common American food item and Colombo Yoghurt was sold to General Mills in 1993.

**Nutritional Value and Health Benefits**

Tzatziki, an appetiser made with yoghurt, popular in Greece and Bulgaria, where it is called Dry Tarator.

Yoghurt is nutritionally rich in protein, calcium, riboflavin, vitamin B6 and vitamin B12. It has nutritional benefits beyond those of milk. People who are moderately lactose-intolerant can enjoy yoghurt without ill effects, because much of the lactose in the milk precursor is converted to lactic acid by the bacterial culture.

Yoghurt also has medical uses, in particular for a variety of gastrointestinal conditions, and in preventing antibiotic-associated diarrhea. One study suggests that eating yoghurt containing *L. acidophilus* helps prevent vulvovaginal candidiasis, though the evidence is not conclusive.

Yoghurt is believed to promote good gum health, possibly because of the probiotic effect of lactic acids present in yoghurt.

A study published in the International Journal of Obesity (11 January 2005) also found that the consumption of low fat yoghurt can promote weight loss. In the trial, obese individuals who ate three servings of low fat yoghurt a day as part of a low calorie diet lost 22 per cent more weight than the control group who only cut back on calories and did not have extra calcium. They also lost 81 per cent more abdominal fat.

To offset its natural sourness, yoghurt can be sold sweetened, flavoured, or in containers with fruit or fruit jam on the bottom. If the fruit has been stirred into the yoghurt before purchase, it is commonly referred to as Swiss-style Most yoghurts in the North America have added pectin, found naturally in fruit, and/or gelatin to artificially create thickness and creaminess at lower cost. This type of adulterated product is also marketed under the name Swiss-style, although it is unrelated to the way yoghurt is eaten in Switzerland. Some specialty yoghurts, often called 'cream line', have a layer of fermented fat at the top. Fruit jam is used instead of raw fruit pieces in fruit yoghurts to allow storage for weeks.

Sweeteners such as cane sugar are often present in large amounts in commercial yoghurt.

Dadiah, or Dadih, is a traditional West Sumatran yoghurt made from water buffalo milk. It is fermented in bamboo tubes.

Yogurt is popular in Nepal, where it is served both as an appetizer or dessert. Locally called *dahi* (???), it is a part of the Nepali culture, used in local festivals, marriage ceremonies, parties, religious occasions, family gatherings, and so on. The most famous type of Nepalese yogurt is called *juju dahu*, originating from the city of Bhaktapur.

Tarator and Cacik are popular cold soups made from yoghurt, popular during summertime in Albania, Bulgaria, Republic of Macedonia, and Turkey. They are made with ayran, cucumbers, dill, salt, olive oil, and optionally garlic and ground walnuts.

Rahmjoghurt, a creamy yoghurt with much higher fat content (10%) than most yoghurts offered in English-speaking countries (*Rahm* is German for 'cream'), is available in Germany and other countries.

Cream top yogurt is yoghurt made with unhomogenized milk. A layer of cream rises to the top, forming a rich yogurt cream with a taste and texture not unlike sour cream. Cream top yoghurt was first made commercially popular in the United States by Brown Cow of Newfield, NY, bucking the trend toward low- and non-fat yoghurts.

Kefir is a slightly alcoholic (up to 0.88%) fermented youghurt originating in the North Caucasus and has been a main food staple in Russia and the other republics of the former Russian Empire.

Matsoni is a yoghurt-like dairy product, popular in Georgia and Armenia. It is started with *Lactococcus lactis subsp. cremoris* and *Acetobacter orientalis* species and has a viscous, honey-like texture. It is milder in taste than other varieties of yoghurts since it is less sour and has less alcohol than kefir.

Matsoni is called 'Caspian Sea Yogurt' in Japan, where it is believed to have been introduced in 1986 by researchers returning from a trip to the Caucasus region of Georgia and Armenia. Ideally, Caspian Sea yoghurt is made at home because it requires neither special equipment nor unobtainable culture. It can be made at room temperature (20-30 °C) in 10 to 15 hours. In Japan, freeze-dried starter cultures are sold in department stores and online, although many people obtain starter cultures from friends.

Jameed is yoghurt which is salted and dried to preserve it. It is popular in Jordan.

Zabady is the yoghurt made in Egypt. It is essentially famous in Ramadan fasting as it is thought to prevent feeling thirst during fasting all day long.

Raita is a yoghurt-based South Asian/Indian condiment, used as a side dish. The yoghurt is seasoned with cilantro (coriander), cumin, mint, cayenne pepper, and other herbs and spices. Vegetables such as cucumber and onions are mixed in. The mixture is served chilled. Raita has a cooling effect on the palate which makes it a good foil for spicy Indian dishes.

[dudh] is a Sindhi-Curd, popular in India. People drink [dudh] along with food at intervals, to help digestion and make food more delicious. At some places [dudh] is also served with plain rice.

*Dahi*, or *Perugu*, is a yoghurt of the Indian subcontinent, known for its characteristic taste and consistency. The word *dahi* seems to be derived from the Sanskrit word *dadhi*, one of the five elixirs, or panchamrita, often used in Hindu ritual.

*Dahi* also holds cultural symbolism in many homes in the *Mithilanchal* region of Bihar. It is found in different flavours, two of which are famous: sour yoghurt (*tauk doi*) and sweet yoghurt (*meesti* or *podi doi*). In India, it is often used in cosmetics mixed with turmeric and honey. Sour yoghurt is also used as a hair conditioner by women in many parts of India. *Dahi* is also known as *Thayiru* (Malayalam), *doi* (Assamese, Bengali), *dohi* (Oriya), *perugu* (Telugu), *Mosaru* (Kannada), *Thayir* (Tamil), or *Srikand*, a popular dessert in India, is made from drained yoghurt, saffron, cardamom, nutmeg and sugar and sometimes fruits such as mango or pineapple.

### Strained Yoghurts and Yoghurt Cheese

Strained yoghurts are types of yoghurt which are strained through a paper or cloth filter, traditionally made of muslin, to remove the whey, giving a much thicker consistency and a distinctive, slightly tangy taste.

Labneh is a strained yoghurt used for sandwiches popular in Arab countries. Olive oil, cucumber slices, olives, and various green herbs may be added. It can be thickened further and rolled into balls, preserved in olive oil, and fermented for a few more weeks. It is sometimes used with onions, meat, and nuts as a stuffing for a variety of pies or kebbeh balls.

Shankleesh is a type of cheese made from cured dried labneh, featured in the gastronomy of Lebanon and surrounding areas. The labneh is salted, dried and rolled into balls. It comes in different varieties ranging from the fresh variant in olive oil and thyme to the 'aged' balls covered with spices.

Some types of strained yoghurts are boiled in open vats first, so that the liquid content is reduced. The popular East Indian dessert, a variation of traditional dahi called mishti dahi, offers a thicker, more custard-like consistency, and is usually sweeter than western yoghurts.

Strained yoghurt is also enjoyed in Greece and is the main component of *tzadziki*, a well-known accompaniment to gyros and souvlaki pita sandwiches.

## Beverages

Ayran or dhalla is a yoghurt-based, salty drink popular in Albania, Bulgaria, Turkey, Azerbaijan, Iran, Republic of Macedonia, Kazakhstan and Kyrgyzstan. It is made by mixing yoghurt with water and (sometimes) salt. The same drink is known as *doogh* in Iran; *tan* in Armenia; *laban ayran* in Syria and Lebanon; *shenina* in Iraq and Jordan; *laban arbil* in Iraq; *majjiga* (Telugu), *majjige* (Kannada), and *moru* (Tamil) in South India; *lassi* in Punjab and all over India. A similar drink, doogh, is popular in the Middle East between Lebanon, Iran and Afghanistan; it differs from ayran by the addition of herbs, usually mint, and is carbonated, commonly with seltzer water.

Lassi is a yoghurt-based beverage originally from the Indian subcontinent that is usually slightly salty or sweet. Lassi is a staple of Punjab. In some parts of the subcontinent, the sweet version may be commercially flavoured with rosewater, mango or other fruit juice to create a very different drink. Salty lassi is usually flavoured with ground, roasted cumin and red chillies; this salty variation may also use buttermilk, and is interchangeably called *ghol* (Bengal), *mattha* (North India), *tak* (Maharashtra), or *chaas* (Gujarat). Lassi is also very widely drunk in Pakistan.

A Central Asian Turco-Mongolian drink made from mare's milk is called *kumis*, or *airag* in Mongolia. Some American dairies have offered a drink called 'kefir' for many years with fruit flavours but without carbonation or alcohol.

Sweetened yoghurt drinks are the usual form in Europe (including UK) and the US, containing fruit and added sweeteners. These are typically called 'drinking/drinkable yoghurt', such as Yop. Also available are 'yoghurt smoothies' which contain a higher proportion of fruit and are more like smoothies.

In Ecuador, yogurt smoothies flavored with native fruit are served with pan de yuca as a common type of fast food establishment.

Milk allergy is a food allergy, an adverse immune reaction to one or more of the proteins in cow's milk and/or the milk of other animals — proteins that are normally harmless to the non-allergic individual.

Milk allergy can cause anaphylaxis, a potentially life-threatening condition.

*Milk allergy is a separate and distinct condition from lactose intolerance.* (Lactose intolerance is considered the normal state for most adults on a worldwide scale and is not typically considered to be a disease condition.

The principal symptoms are gastrointestinal, dermatological and respiratory. These can translate to: skin rash, hives, vomiting, and gastric distress such as diarrhoea, constipation, stomach pain or flatulence). The clinical spectrum extends to diverse disorders: anaphylactic reactions, atopic dermatitis, wheeze, infantile colic, gastroesophageal reflux (GER), oesophagitis, allergic colitis headache/migraine and constipation.

The symptoms may occur within a few minutes after exposure in *immediate reactions*, or after hours (and in some cases after several days) in *delayed reactions*.

## Difference Between Milk Allergy and Lactose Intolerance

Milk allergy is a food allergy, an adverse immune reaction to a food protein that is normally harmless to the non-allergic individual. Lactose intolerance is a non-allergic food sensitivity, and comes from a lack of production of the enzyme lactase, required to digest the predominant sugar in milk. Lactose intolerance is not actually a disease or malady. Adverse effects of lactose intolerance occur at much higher milk consumption than adverse effects of milk allergy.

## Difference from Milk Protein Intolerance

Milk protein intolerance (MPI) is delayed reaction to a food protein that is normally harmless to the non-allergic, non-intolerant individual. Milk protein intolerance produces a non-IgE antibody and is not detected by allergy blood tests. Milk protein intolerance produces a range of symptoms very similar to milk allergy symptoms, but can also include blood and/or mucus in the stool. Treatment for milk protein intolerance is the same as for milk allergy. Milk protein intolerance is also referred to as milk soy protein intolerance (MSPI).

## Treatment

Currently the only treatment for milk allergies is total avoidance of milk proteins. Products in addition to milk itself to be avoided by those with milk allergy include yogurt, butter, cheese, and cream. Goats' milk products may also need to be avoided.

Ingredients that also denote that food product contains dairy milk include whey, casein, caseinate, butter flavour, lactic acid (lactic acid derived from dairy products), natural or artificial flavors such as milk or butter flavor, and sodium caseinate.

It is commonplace for milk or milk derivatives to be included in processed foods such as bread, crackers, cookies, cakes, prepared meats, 'soy cheese', soups, gravies, crisps, margarine, and products labelled 'non-dairy', such as whipped topping and creamer (non-dairy simply means less than 0.5 per cent milk by weight.

Also, many processed foods that do not contain milk may be processed on equipment contaminated with dairy foods, which may cause an allergic reaction in some sensitive individuals.

## Milk Avoidance and Replacement for Infants

Since milk protein may be transferred from a breastfeeding mother to an allergic infant, lactating mothers are put on a dairy elimination diet. For formula fed infants, milk substitute formulas are used to provide a complete source of nutrition. Milk substitutes include soy based formulas, hypoallergenic formulas based on partially or extensively hydrolyzed protein (such as Nutramigen, Alimentum, and Pregestimil), and free amino acid-based formulas (such as Neocate, EleCare, and Nutramigen AA).

Soy based formula does have a risk of allergic sensitivity, as some infants who are allergic to milk may also be allergic to soy.

Hydrolyzed formulas come in partially hydrolyzed and extensively hydrolyzed varieties. Partially hydrolyzed formulas (PHFs) are characterized by a larger proportion of long chain peptides and are considered more palatable. However, they are intended for milder cases and are not considered suitable for treatment of moderate to severe milk allergy or intolerance. Extensively hydrolyzed formulas (EHFs) are comprised of proteins that have been largely broken down into free amino acids and short peptides. Casein and whey are the most commonly used sources of protein in hydrolyzed formulas because of their high nutritional quality and their amino acid composition.

Non-milk derived amino acid-based formulas, also known as elemental formulas, are suitable for the treatment of mild, moderate, and severe milk allergy in infants that exhibit allergic reactions to partially and extensively hydrolyzed formulas.

### Milk Substitution for Children and Adults

There are many commercially available replacements for milk for children and adults — Rice milk, soy milk, oat milk and almond milk are also sometimes used as milk substitutes, but are not suitable nutrition for infants. However, special infant formula based on soy, rice, almonds or carob seeds is commercially available. Fruit juices supplemented with calcium which may provide an alternative for adults and children. If on an avoidance diet, it is important that dietary advice is taken as a replacement source of calcium may need to be found to prevent the longer term risk of calcium deficiency and osteoporosis. Very good dietary sources of calcium are for example sesame seeds, hemp seeds and some kinds of tofu.

### Accidental Exposure

Treatment for accidental ingestion of milk products by allergic individuals varies depending on the sensitivity of the allergic person. Frequently medications such as an Epinephrine pen or an Antihistamine such as Diphenhydramine (Benadryl) are prescribed by an allergist in case of accidental ingestion. Milk allergy can cause anaphylaxis, a severe, life threatening allergic reaction.

Like many food allergies milk allergy may be outgrown eventually by children, although a percentage of children do not outgrow their allergy. Milk allergy is more likely to be outgrown than peanut allergy.

### Vaccines

Some vaccines contain casamino acid, derived from bovine casein, as the growth medium: Casamino acid is a mixture of amino acids derived from the hydrolysis of casein, used as a supplement in the growth media. The FDA does not require allergen labelling on medications or vaccines and most doctors are unaware of this ingredient. Extreme caution must be taken to prevent a serious or life threatening reaction.

### Statistics

Milk allergy is the most common food allergy in early childhood. It affects somewhere between 2 per cent and 3 per cent of infants in developed countries, but approximately 85-90 per cent of affected children lose clinical reactivity to milk once they surpass 3 years of age.

Between 13 per cent and 20 per cent of children allergic to milk are also allergic to beef.

### Fat

Fats consist of a wide group of compounds that are generally soluble in organic solvents and largely insoluble in water. Chemically, fats are generally triesters of glycerol and fatty acids. Fats may be either solid or liquid at room temperature, depending on their structure and composition. Although the words 'oils', 'fats', and 'lipids' are all used to refer to fats, 'oils' is usually used to refer to fats that are liquids at normal room temperature, while 'fats' is usually used to refer to fats that are solids at normal room temperature. 'Lipids' is used to refer to both liquid and solid fats, along with other related substances. The word 'oil' is used for any substance that does not mix with water and has a greasy feel, such as petroleum (or crude oil) and heating oil, regardless of its chemical structure

Fats form a category of lipid, distinguished from other lipids by their chemical structure and physical properties. This category of molecules is important for many forms of life, serving both structural and metabolic functions. They are an important part of the diet of most heterotrophs (including humans). Fats or lipids are broken down in the body by enzymes called lipases produced in the pancreas.

Examples of edible animal fats are lard (pig fat), fish oil, and butter or ghee. They are obtained from fats in the milk, meat and under the skin of the animal. Examples of edible plant fats are peanut, soya bean, sunflower, sesame, coconut, olive, and vegetable oils. Margarine and vegetable shortening, which can be derived from the above oils, are used mainly for baking. These examples of fats can be categorized into saturated fats and unsaturated fats.

There are many different kinds of fats, but each is a variation on the same chemical structure. All fats consist of fatty acids (chains of carbon and hydrogen atoms, with a carboxylic acid group at one end) bonded to a backbone structure, often glycerol (a 'backbone' of carbon, hydrogen, and oxygen). Chemically, this is a triester of glycerol, an ester being the molecule formed from the reaction of the carboxylic acid and an organic alcohol. As a simple visual illustration, if the kinks and angles of these chains were straightened out, the molecule would have the shape of a capital letter E. The fatty acids would each be a horizontal line; the glycerol 'backbone' would be the vertical line that joins the horizontal lines. Fats therefore have 'ester' bonds.

The properties of any specific fat molecule depend on the particular fatty acids that constitute it. Different fatty acids are composed of different numbers of carbon and hydrogen atoms. The carbon atoms, each bonded to two neighboring carbon atoms, form a zigzagging chain; the more carbon atoms there are in any fatty acid, the longer its chain will be. Fatty acids with long chains are more susceptible to intermolecular forces of attraction (in this case, van der Waals forces), raising its melting point. Long chains also yield more energy per molecule when metabolized.

A fat's constituent fatty acids may also differ in the number of hydrogen atoms that are bonded to the chain of carbon atoms. Each carbon atom is typically bonded to two hydrogen atoms. When a fatty acid has this typical arrangement, it is called 'saturated', because the carbon atoms are saturated with hydrogen; meaning they are bonded to as many hydrogens as possible. In other fats, a carbon atom may instead bond to only one other hydrogen atom, and have a double bond to a neighbouring carbon atom. This results in an 'unsaturated' fatty acid. More specifically, it would be a 'monounsaturated' fatty acid, whereas, a 'polyunsaturated' fatty acid would be a fatty acid with more than one double bond. Saturated and unsaturated fats differ in their energy content and melting point. Since an unsaturated fat contains fewer carbon-hydrogen bonds than a saturated fat with the same number of carbon atoms, unsaturated fats will yield slightly less energy during metabolism than saturated fats with the same number of carbon atoms. Saturated fats can stack themselves in a closely packed arrangement, so they can freeze easily and are typically solid at room temperature. But the rigid double bond in an unsaturated fat fundamentally changes the chemistry of the fat. There are two ways the double bond may be arranged: the isomer with both parts of the chain on the same side of the double bond (the *cis*-isomer), or the isomer with the parts of the chain on opposite sides of the double bond (the *trans*-isomer). Most *trans*-isomer fats (commonly called trans fats) are commercially produced rather than naturally occurring. The *cis*-isomer introduces a kink into the molecule that prevents the fats from stacking efficiently as in the case of fats with saturated chains. This decreases intermolecular forces between the fat molecules, making it more difficult for unsaturated cis-fats to freeze; they are typically liquid at room temperature. Trans fats may still stack like saturated fats, and are not as susceptible to metabolization as other fats. Trans fats may significantly increase the risk of coronary heart disease.

## Importance for Living Organisms

Vitamins A, D, E, and K are fat-soluble, meaning they can only be digested, absorbed, and transported in conjunction with fats. Fats are also sources of essential fatty acids, an important dietary requirement.

Fats play a vital role in maintaining healthy skin and hair, insulating body organs against shock, maintaining body temperature, and promoting healthy cell function.

Fats also serve as energy stores for the body, containing about 37.8 kilojoules (9 Calories) per gram of fat . They are broken down in the body to release glycerol and free fatty acids. The glycerol can be converted to glucose by the liver and thus used as a source of energy.

Fat also serves as a useful buffer towards a host of diseases. When a particular substance, whether chemical or biotic – reaches unsafe levels in the bloodstream, the body can effectively dilute — or at least maintain equilibrium of – the offending substances by storing it in new fat tissue. This helps to protect vital organs, until such time as the offending substances can be metabolized and/or removed from the body by such means as excretion, urination, accidental or intentional bloodletting, sebum excretion, and hair growth.

While it is nearly impossible to remove fat completely from the diet, it would be unhealthy to do so. Some fatty acids are essential nutrients, meaning that they can't be produced in the body from other compounds and need to be consumed in small amounts. All other fats required by the body are non-essential and can be produced in the body from other compounds.

**Adipose Tissue**

The obese mouse on the left has large stores of adipose tissue. For comparison, a mouse with a normal amount of adipose tissue is shown on the right.

In animals, adipose, or fatty tissue is the body's means of storing metabolic energy over extended periods of time. Depending on current physiological conditions, adipocytes store fat derived from the diet and liver metabolism or degrade stored fat to supply fatty acids and glycerol to the circulation. These metabolic activities are regulated by several hormones (i.e., insulin, glucagon and epinephrine). The location of the tissue determines its metabolic profile: 'Visceral fat' is located within the abdominal wall (i.e., beneath the wall of abdominal muscle) whereas 'subcutaneous fat' is located beneath the skin (and includes fat that is located in the abdominal area beneath the skin but *above* the abdominal muscle wall). Visceral fat was recently discovered to be a significant producer of signaling chemicals (ie, hormones), among which are several which are involved in inflammatory tissue responses. One of these is resistin which has been linked to obesity, insulin resistance, and type 2 diabetes. This latter result is currently controversial, and there have been reputable studies supporting all sides on the issue.

11

# Dried Milk

Dried milk (Milk Powder) products play a significant role in conserving the milk solids since their biological value can be retained for a long period of time under relatively simple storage conditions. The roller dried powder finds special application in the manufacture of infant foods, confectionery, ice cream, milk sweets etc.

Milk is concentrated by means of condensation to about 20-25 per cent of total solids in a vacuum pan or evaporator and fed to continuously revolving drum drier, which are internally heated with steam. The film of the dried product is continuously scrapped off by a stationary knife or doctor blade, located opposite in the point of application of milk round, which is then sifted, packed.

## Method of Manufacture of Dried Milk

- The milk is separated (in case of skim milk powder) or clarified and standardized (in case of whole milk powder).
- The milk is fore-warmed to 95°C and re-condensed to 20 per cent total solids. Homogenization of the condensed milk is done in case of manufacture of whole milk powder.

The roller drums are observed for its correct alignment with the knife, cleanliness of the surface of the rollers,

The semi dried and charred powders obtained initially have to be discarded. The conveyors are adjusted properly to carry the powder.

When the milk flow is over, the conveyors are stopped and some hot water is run over the drums.

The knife is taken off from the surface of the drum and supply of steam to the drum is cut.

## Spray Dried Milk Powder

Spray drying is the most important method of drying milk and milk products. By spraying in to a stream of hot air, the droplets formed present an extremely large amount of surface area and get dried immediately due to rapid evaporation of moisture. Milk is preheated and concentrated to 40-45 per cent per cent total solids.

Hot air is filtered and directed in to the drying chamber. The concentrate is atomized to obtain small particles ranging from 10-100m in diameter. The air leaving the drying chamber enters a cyclone separator where the fine particles are collected. The dried products are cooled, sifted and packed in suitable packaging material.

## Method of Manufacture of Spray Dried Milk Powder

The milk is separated (in case of skim milk powder) or clarified and standardized (in case of whole milk powder).

The milk is fore-warmed to 95°C and re-condensed to 40 per cent total solids. Homogenization of the condensed milk is done in case of manufacture of whole milk powder.

The spray drier is cleaned, pipelines are connected and general conditions of the valves and cyclone separators are checked.

The steam is let in to the air heating coils. The exhaust fan is switched on, keeping the main door partially open.

The blower is started and the main door is closed.

The temperature of the hot air is adjusted to 180°C and this temperature is maintained for ten minutes to ensure the sterility of the unit.

The atomizer is started and allowed to obtain the required speed.

Initially, 20 litres of water is used for spraying through the feed pump.

When the outlet air temperature reaches 100°C, the feed is changed to concentrate. The temperature of the inlet air entering the drying chamber usually ranges from 150-260°C and the outlet air exhausted from the drying chamber ranges from 100-105°C. the relative humidity of the drying chamber is quite low i.e. 3-4 per cent.

The *milk powder* is collected in the powder silo.

When the flow of milk is over, the balance tank is flushed with about 20 litres of hot water (90°C) and the flow of milk to the dryer is reduced immediately.

The atomizer and feed pump are stopped when the feed is empty.

The steam supply to the air heating coils is stopped.

The exhaust fan and air blower are stopped.

The dried milk or milk powder is packed in required quantity in suitable containers.

## Protein

Proteins (also known as polypeptides) are organic compounds made of amino acids arranged in a linear chain and folded into a globular form. The amino acids in a polymer are joined together by the peptide bonds between the carboxyl and amino groups of adjacent amino acid residues. The sequence of amino acids in a protein is defined by the sequence of a gene, which is encoded in the genetic code. In general, the genetic code specifies 20 standard amino acids; however, in certain organisms the genetic code can include selenocysteine — and in certain archaea — pyrrolysine. Shortly after or even during synthesis, the residues in a protein are often chemically modified by post-translational modification, which alters the physical and chemical properties, folding, stability, activity, and ultimately, the function of the proteins. Proteins can also work together to achieve a particular function, and they often associate to form stable complexes.

Like other biological macromolecules such as polysaccharides and nucleic acids, proteins are essential parts of organisms and participate in virtually every process within cells. Many proteins are enzymes that catalyze biochemical reactions and are vital to metabolism. Proteins also have structural or mechanical functions, such as actin and myosin in muscle and the proteins in the cytoskeleton, which form a system of scaffolding that maintains cell shape. Other proteins are important in cell signaling, immune responses, cell adhesion, and the cell cycle. Proteins are also necessary in animals' diets, since animals cannot synthesize all the amino acids they need and must obtain essential amino acids from food. Through the process of digestion, animals break down ingested protein into free amino acids that are then used in metabolism.

Proteins were first described by the Dutch chemist Gerhardus Johannes Mulder and named by the Swedish chemist Jöns Jakob Berzelius in 1838. The central role of proteins in living organisms was however not fully appreciated until 1926, when James B. Sumner showed that the enzyme urease was a protein. The first protein to be sequenced was insulin, by Frederick Sanger, who won the Nobel Prize for this achievement in 1958. The first protein structures to be solved were hemoglobin and myoglobin, by Max Perutz and Sir John Cowdery Kendrew, respectively, in 1958. The three-dimensional structures of both proteins were first determined by x-ray diffraction analysis; Perutz and

Kendrew shared the 1962 Nobel Prize in Chemistry for these discoveries. Proteins may be purified from other cellular components using a variety of techniques such as ultracentrifugation, precipitation, electrophoresis, and chromatography; the advent of genetic engineering has made possible a number of methods to facilitate purification. Methods commonly used to study protein structure and function include immunohistochemistry, site-directed mutagenesis, and mass spectrometry.

Most proteins are linear polymers built from series of up to 20 different L-a-amino acids. All amino acids possess common structural features, including an a-carbon to which an amino group, a carboxyl group, and a variable side chain are bonded. Only proline differs from this basic structure as it contains an unusual ring to the N-end amine group, which forces the CO–NH amide moiety into a fixed conformation. The side chains of the standard amino acids, detailed in the list of standard amino acids, have a great variety of chemical structures and properties; it is the combined effect of all of the amino acid side chains in a protein that ultimately determines its three-dimensional structure and its chemical reactivity.

The amino acids in a polypeptide chain are linked by peptide bonds. Once linked in the protein chain, an individual amino acid is called a *residue,* and the linked series of carbon, nitrogen, and oxygen atoms are known as the *main chain* or *protein backbone.* The peptide bond has two resonance forms that contribute some double-bond character and inhibit rotation around its axis, so that the alpha carbons are roughly coplanar. The other two dihedral angles in the peptide bond determine the local shape assumed by the protein backbone. The end of the protein with a free carboxyl group is known as the C-terminus or carboxy terminus, whereas the end with a free amino group is known as the N-terminus or amino terminus.

The words *protein*, *polypeptide*, and *peptide* are a little ambiguous and can overlap in meaning. *Protein* is generally used to refer to the complete biological molecule in a stable conformation, whereas *peptide* is generally reserved for a short amino acid oligomers often lacking a stable three-dimensional structure. However, the boundary between the two is not well defined and usually lies near 20-30 residues. *Polypeptide* can refer to any single linear chain of amino acids, usually regardless of length, but often implies an absence of a defined conformation.

Proteins are assembled from amino acids using information encoded in genes. Each protein has its own unique amino acid sequence that is specified by the nucleotide sequence of the gene encoding this protein. The genetic code is a set of three-nucleotide sets called codons and each three-nucleotide combination designates an amino acid, for example AUG (adenine-uracil-guanine) is the code for methionine. Because DNA contains four nucleotides, the total number of possible codons is 64; hence, there is some redundancy in the genetic code, with some amino acids specified by more than one codon. Genes encoded in DNA are first transcribed into pre-messenger RNA (mRNA) by proteins such as RNA polymerase. Most organisms then process the pre-mRNA (also known as a *primary transcript*) using various forms of post-transcriptional modification to form the mature mRNA, which is then used as a template for protein synthesis by the ribosome. In prokaryotes the mRNA may either be used as soon as it is produced, or be bound by a ribosome after having moved away from the nucleoid. In contrast, eukaryotes make mRNA in the cell nucleus and then translocate it across the nuclear membrane into the cytoplasm, where protein synthesis then takes place. The rate of protein synthesis is higher in prokaryotes than eukaryotes and can reach up to 20 amino acids per second.

The process of synthesizing a protein from an mRNA template is known as translation. The mRNA is loaded onto the ribosome and is read three nucleotides at a time by matching each codon to its base pairing anticodon located on a transfer RNA molecule, which carries the amino acid corresponding to the codon it recognizes. The enzyme aminoacyl tRNA synthetase 'charges' the tRNA molecules with the correct amino acids. The growing polypeptide is often termed the *nascent chain*. Proteins are always biosynthesized from N-terminus to C-terminus.

The size of a synthesized protein can be measured by the number of amino acids it contains and by its total molecular mass, which is normally reported in units of *daltons* (synonymous with atomic mass units), or the derivative unit kilodalton (kDa). Yeast proteins are on average 466 amino acids long and 53 kDa in mass. The largest known proteins are the titins, a component of the muscle sarcomere, with a molecular mass of almost 3,000 kDa and a total length of almost 27,000 amino acids.

Short proteins can also be synthesized chemically by a family of methods known as peptide synthesis, which rely on organic synthesis techniques such as chemical ligation to produce peptides in high yield. Chemical synthesis allows for the introduction of non-natural amino acids into polypeptide chains, such as attachment of fluorescent probes to amino acid side chains. These methods are useful in laboratory biochemistry and cell biology, though generally not for commercial applications. Chemical synthesis is inefficient for polypeptides longer than about 300 amino acids, and the synthesized proteins may not readily assume their native tertiary structure. Most chemical synthesis methods proceed from C-terminus to N-terminus, opposite the biological reaction.

Most proteins fold into unique 3-dimensional structures. The shape into which a protein naturally folds is known as its native conformation Although many proteins can fold unassisted, simply through the chemical properties of their amino acids, others require the aid of molecular chaperones to fold into their native states. Biochemists often refer to four distinct aspects of a protein's structure:

- *Primary structure*: the amino acid sequence.
- *Secondary structure*: regularly repeating local structures stabilized by hydrogen bonds. The most common examples are the alpha helix, beta sheet and turns. Because secondary structures are local, many regions of different secondary structure can be present in the same protein molecule.
- *Tertiary structure*: the overall shape of a single protein molecule; the spatial relationship of the secondary structures to one another. Tertiary structure is generally stabilized by nonlocal interactions, most commonly the formation of a hydrophobic core, but also through salt bridges, hydrogen bonds, disulfide bonds, and even post-translational modifications. The term 'tertiary structure" is often used as synonymous with the term *fold*. The Tertiary structure is what controls the basic function of the protein.
- *Quaternary structure*: the structure formed by several protein molecules (polypeptide chains), usually called *protein subunits* in this context, which function as a single protein complex.

Proteins are not entirely rigid molecules. In addition to these levels of structure, proteins may shift between several related structures while they perform their functions. In the context of these functional rearrangements, these tertiary or quaternary structures are usually referred to as 'conformations', and transitions between them are called *conformational changes*. Such changes are often induced by the binding of a substrate molecule to an enzyme's active site, or the physical region of the protein that participates in chemical catalysis. In solution proteins also undergo variation in structure through thermal vibration and the collision with other molecules.

Molecular surface of several proteins showing their comparative sizes. From left to right are: immunoglobulin

G (IgG, an antibody), hemoglobin, insulin (a hormone), adenylate kinase (an enzyme), and glutamine synthetase (an enzyme).

Proteins can be informally divided into three main classes, which correlate with typical tertiary structures: globular proteins, fibrous proteins, and membrane proteins. Almost all globular proteins are soluble and many are enzymes. Fibrous proteins are often structural, such as collagen, the major component of connective tissue, or keratin, the protein component of hair and nails. Membrane proteins often serve as receptors or provide channels for polar or charged molecules to pass through the cell membrane.

A special case of intramolecular hydrogen bonds within proteins, poorly shielded from water attack and hence promoting their own dehydration, are called dehydrons.

Discovering the tertiary structure of a protein, or the quaternary structure of its complexes, can provide important clues about how the protein performs its function. Common experimental methods of structure determination include X-ray crystallography and NMR spectroscopy, both of which can produce information at atomic resolution. Dual polarisation interferometry is a quantitative analytical method for measuring the overall protein conformation and conformational changes due to interactions or other stimulus. Circular dichroism is another laboratory technique for determining internal beta sheet/helical composition of proteins. Cryoelectron microscopy is used to produce lower-resolution structural information about very large protein complexes, including assembled viruses; a variant known as electron crystallography can also produce high-resolution information in some cases , especially for two-dimensional crystals of membrane proteins. Solved structures are usually deposited in the Protein Data Bank (PDB), a freely available resource from which structural data about thousands of proteins can be obtained in the form of Cartesian coordinates for each atom in the protein.

Many more gene sequences are known than protein structures. Further, the set of solved structures is biased toward proteins that can be easily subjected to the conditions required in X-ray crystallography, one of the major structure determination methods. In particular, globular proteins are comparatively easy to crystallize in preparation for X-ray crystallography. Membrane proteins, by contrast, are difficult to crystallize and are underrepresented in the PDB. Structural genomics initiatives have attempted to remedy these deficiencies by systematically solving representative structures of major fold classes. Protein structure prediction methods attempt to provide a means of generating a plausible structure for proteins whose structures have not been experimentally determined.

Proteins are the chief actors within the cell, said to be carrying out the duties specified by the information encoded in genes. With the exception of certain types of RNA, most other biological molecules are relatively inert elements upon which proteins act. Proteins make up half the dry weight of an *Escherichia coli* cell, whereas other macromolecules such as DNA and RNA make up only 3 per cent and 20 per cent, respectively. The set of proteins expressed in a particular cell or cell type is known as its proteome.

The chief characteristic of proteins that also allows their diverse set of functions is their ability to bind other molecules specifically and tightly. The region of the protein responsible for binding another molecule is known as the binding site and is often a depression or 'pocket' on the molecular surface. This binding ability is mediated by the tertiary structure of the protein, which defines the binding site pocket, and by the chemical properties of the surrounding amino acids' side chains. Protein binding can be extraordinarily tight and specific; for example, the ribonuclease inhibitor protein binds to human angiogenin with a sub-femtomolar dissociation constant ($<10^{-15}$ M) but does not bind at all to its amphibian homolog onconase

(>1 M). Extremely minor chemical changes such as the addition of a single methyl group to a binding partner can sometimes suffice to nearly eliminate binding; for example, the aminoacyl tRNA synthetase specific to the amino acid valine discriminates against the very similar side chain of the amino acid isoleucine.

Proteins can bind to other proteins as well as to small-molecule substrates. When proteins bind specifically to other copies of the same molecule, they can oligomerize to form fibrils; this process occurs often in structural proteins that consist of globular monomers that self-associate to form rigid fibers. Protein–protein interactions also regulate enzymatic activity, control progression through the cell cycle, and allow the assembly of large protein complexes that carry out many closely related reactions with a common biological function. Proteins can also bind to, or even be integrated into, cell membranes. The ability of binding partners to induce conformational changes in proteins allows the construction of enormously complex signaling networks. Importantly, as interactions between proteins are reversible, and depend heavily on the availability of different groups of partner proteins to form aggregates that are capable to carry out discrete sets of function, study of the interactions between specific proteins is a key to understand important aspects of cellular function, and ultimately the properties that distinguish particular cell types.

The best-known role of proteins in the cell is as enzymes, which catalyze chemical reactions. Enzymes are usually highly specific and accelerate only one or a few chemical reactions. Enzymes carry out most of the reactions involved in metabolism, as well as manipulating DNA in processes such as DNA replication, DNA repair, and transcription. Some enzymes act on other proteins to add or remove chemical groups in a process known as post-translational modification. About 4,000 reactions are known to be catalyzed by enzymes. The rate acceleration conferred by enzymatic catalysis is often enormous — as much as $10^{17}$-fold increase in rate over the uncatalyzed reaction in the case of orotate decarboxylase (78 million years without the enzyme, 18 milliseconds with the enzyme).

The molecules bound and acted upon by enzymes are called substrates. Although enzymes can consist of hundreds of amino acids, it is usually only a small fraction of the residues that come in contact with the substrate, and an even smaller fraction — 3 to 4 residues on average — that are directly involved in catalysis. The region of the enzyme that binds the substrate and contains the catalytic residues is known as the active site.

Antibodies are protein components of adaptive immune system whose main function is to bind antigens, or foreign substances in the body, and target them for destruction. Antibodies can be secreted into the extracellular environment or anchored in the membranes of specialized B cells known as plasma cells. Whereas enzymes are limited in their binding affinity for their substrates by the necessity of conducting their reaction, antibodies have no such constraints. An antibody's binding affinity to its target is extraordinarily high.

Many ligand transport proteins bind particular small biomolecules and transport them to other locations in the body of a multicellular organism. These proteins must have a high binding affinity when their ligand is present in high concentrations, but must also release the ligand when it is present at low concentrations in the target tissues. The canonical example of a ligand-binding protein is haemoglobin, which transports oxygen from the lungs to other organs and tissues in all vertebrates and has close homologs in every biological kingdom. Lectins are sugar-binding proteins which are highly specific for their sugar moieties. Lectins typically play a role in biological recognition phenomena involving cells and proteins. Receptors and hormones are highly specific binding proteins.

Transmembrane proteins can also serve as ligand transport proteins that alter the permeability of the cell membrane to small molecules and ions. The membrane alone has a hydrophobic core through which polar or charged molecules cannot diffuse. Membrane proteins contain internal channels that allow such molecules to enter and exit the cell. Many ion channel proteins are specialized to select for only a particular ion; for example, potassium and sodium channels often discriminate for only one of the two ions.

## Structural Proteins

Structural proteins confer stiffness and rigidity to otherwise-fluid biological components. Most structural proteins are fibrous proteins; for example, actin and tubulin are globular and soluble as monomers, but polymerize to form long, stiff fibers that comprise the cytoskeleton, which allows the cell to maintain its shape and size. Collagen and elastin are critical components of connective tissue such as cartilage, and keratin is found in hard or filamentous structures such as hair, nails, feathers, hooves, and some animal shells.

Other proteins that serve structural functions are motor proteins such as myosin, kinesin, and dynein, which are capable of generating mechanical forces. These proteins are crucial for cellular motility of single celled organisms and the sperm of many multicellular organisms which reproduce sexually. They also generate the forces exerted by contracting muscles.

## Methods of Study

As some of the most commonly studied biological molecules, the activities and structures of proteins are examined both *in vitro* and *in vivo*. *In vitro* studies of purified proteins in controlled environments are useful for learning how a protein carries out its function: for example, enzyme kinetics studies explore the chemical mechanism of an enzyme's catalytic activity and its relative affinity for various possible substrate molecules. By contrast, *in vivo* experiments on proteins' activities within cells or even within whole organisms can provide complementary information about where a protein functions and how it is regulated.

In order to perform *in vitro* analysis, a protein must be purified away from other cellular components. This process usually begins with cell lysis, in which a cell's membrane is disrupted and its internal contents released into a solution known as a crude lysate. The resulting mixture can be purified using ultracentrifugation, which fractionates the various cellular components into fractions containing soluble proteins; membrane lipids and proteins; cellular organelles, and nucleic acids. Precipitation by a method known as salting out can concentrate the proteins from this lysate. Various types of chromatography are then used to isolate the protein or proteins of interest based on properties such as molecular weight, net charge and binding affinity. The level of purification can be monitored using various types of gel electrophoresis if the desired protein's molecular weight and isoelectric point are known, by spectroscopy if the protein has distinguishable spectroscopic features, or by enzyme assays if the protein has enzymatic activity. Additionally, proteins can be isolated according their charge using electrofocusing.

For natural proteins, a series of purification steps may be necessary to obtain protein sufficiently pure for laboratory applications. To simplify this process, genetic engineering is often used to add chemical features to proteins that make them easier to purify without affecting their structure or activity. Here, a 'tag' consisting of a specific amino acid sequence, often a series of histidine residues (a 'His-tag'), is attached to one terminus of the protein. As a result, when the lysate is passed over a chromatography column containing nickel, the histidine residues ligate the nickel and attach to the column while the untagged components of the lysate pass unimpeded. A number of different tags have been developed to help researchers purify specific proteins from complex mixtures.

The study of proteins *in vivo* is often concerned with the synthesis and localization of the protein within the cell. Although many intracellular proteins are synthesized in the cytoplasm and membrane-bound or secreted proteins in the endoplasmic reticulum, the specifics of how proteins are targeted to specific organelles or cellular structures is often unclear. A useful technique for assessing cellular localization uses genetic engineering to express in a cell a fusion protein or chimera consisting of the natural protein of interest linked to a 'reporter' such as green fluorescent protein (GFP) The fused protein's position within the cell can be cleanly and efficiently visualized using microscopy, as shown in the figure opposite.

Other methods for elucidating the cellular location of proteins requires the use of known compartmental markers for regions such as the ER, the Golgi, lysosomes/vacuoles, mitochondria, chloroplasts, plasma membrane, etc. With the use of fluorescently-tagged versions of these markers or of antibodies to known markers, it becomes much simpler to identify the localization of a protein of interest. For example, indirect immunofluorescence will allow for fluorescence colocalization and demonstration of location. Fluorescent dyes are used to label cellular compartments for a similar purpose.

Other possibilities exist, as well. For example, immunohistochemistry usually utilizes an antibody to one or more proteins of interest that are conjugated to enzymes yielding either luminescent or chromogenic signals that can be compared between samples, allowing for localization information. Another applicable technique is cofractionation in sucrose (or other material) gradients using isopycnic centrifugation. While this technique does not prove colocalization of a compartment of known density and the protein of interest, it does increase the likelihood, and is more amenable to large-scale studies.

Finally, the gold-standard method of cellular localization is immunoelectron microscopy. This technique also uses an antibody to the protein of interest, along with classical electron microscopy techniques. The sample is prepared for normal electron microscopic examination, and then treated with an antibody to the protein of interest that is conjugated to an extremely electro-dense material, usually gold. This allows for the localization of both ultrastructural details as well as the protein of interest.

Through another genetic engineering application known as site-directed mutagenesis, researchers can alter the protein sequence and hence its structure, cellular localization, and susceptibility to regulation. This technique even allows the incorporation of unnatural amino acids into proteins, using modified tRNAs, and may allow the rational design of new proteins with novel properties.

## Proteomics and Bioinformatics

The total complement of proteins present at a time in a cell or cell type is known as its proteome, and the study of such large-scale data sets defines the field of proteomics, named by analogy to the related field of genomics. Key experimental techniques in proteomics include 2D electrophoresis, which allows the separation of a large number of proteins, mass spectrometry, which allows rapid high-throughput identification of proteins and sequencing of peptides (most often after in-gel digestion), protein microarrays, which allow the detection of the relative levels of a large number of proteins present in a cell, and two-hybrid screening, which allows the systematic exploration of protein-protein interactions. The total complement of biologically possible such interactions is known as the interactome. A systematic attempt to determine the structures of proteins representing every possible fold is known as structural genomics.

The large amount of genomic and proteomic data available for a variety of organisms, including the human genome, allows researchers to efficiently identify homologous proteins in distantly related organisms by sequence alignment. Sequence profiling tools can perform more specific sequence manipulations such as restriction enzyme maps, open reading frame analyses for nucleotide sequences, and secondary structure prediction. From this data phylogenetic trees can be constructed and evolutionary hypotheses developed using special software like ClustalW regarding the ancestry of modern organisms and the genes they express. The field of bioinformatics seeks to assemble, annotate, and analyze genomic and proteomic data, applying computational techniques to biological problems such as gene finding and cladistics.

Complementary to the field of structural genomics, protein structure prediction seeks to develop efficient ways to provide plausible models for proteins whose structures have not yet been determined experimentally. The most successful type of structure prediction, known as homology modeling, relies on the existence of a 'template' structure with sequence similarity to the protein being modeled; structural genomics' goal is to provide sufficient representation in solved structures to model most of those that remain. Although producing accurate models remains a challenge when only distantly related template structures are available, it has been suggested that sequence alignment is the bottleneck in this process, as quite accurate models can be produced if a 'perfect' sequence alignment is known. Many structure prediction methods have served to inform the emerging field of protein engineering, in which novel protein folds have already been designed. A more complex computational problem is the prediction of intermolecular interactions, such as in molecular docking and protein–protein interaction prediction.

The processes of protein folding and binding can be simulated using such technique as molecular mechanics, in particular, molecular dynamics and Monte Carlo, which increasingly take advantage of parallel and distributed computing; molecular modeling on GPU). The folding of small alpha-helical protein domains such as the villin headpiece and the HIV accessory protein have been successfully simulated *in silico*, and hybrid methods that combine standard molecular dynamics with quantum mechanics calculations have allowed exploration of the electronic states of rhodopsins.

Most microorganisms and plants can biosynthesize all 20 standard amino acids, while animals (including humans) must obtain some of the amino acids from the diet. The amino acids that an organism cannot synthesize on its own are referred to as essential amino acids. Key enzymes that synthesize certain amino acids are not present in animals — such as aspartokinase, which catalyzes the first step in the synthesis of lysine, methionine, and threonine from aspartate. If amino acids are present in the environment, microorganisms can conserve energy by taking up the amino acids from their surroundings and downregulating their biosynthetic pathways.

In animals, amino acids are obtained through the consumption of foods containing protein. Ingested proteins are broken down through digestion, which typically involves denaturation of the protein through exposure to acid and hydrolysis by enzymes called proteases. Some ingested amino acids are used for protein biosynthesis, while others are converted to glucose through gluconeogenesis, or fed into the citric acid cycle. This use of protein as a fuel is particularly important under starvation conditions as it allows the body's own proteins to be used to support life, particularly those found in muscle. Amino acids are also an important dietary source of nitrogen.

## History and Etymology

Proteins were recognized as a distinct class of biological molecules in the eighteenth century by Antoine Fourcroy and others, distinguished by the molecules' ability to coagulate or flocculate under treatments with heat or acid. Noted examples at the time included albumin from egg whites, blood serum albumin, fibrin, and wheat gluten. Dutch chemist Gerhardus Johannes Mulder carried out elemental analysis of common proteins and found that nearly all proteins had the same empirical formula, $C_{400}H_{620}N_{100}O_{120}P_1S_1$. He came to the erroneous conclusion that they might be composed of a single type of (very large) molecule. The term 'protein' to describe these molecules was proposed in 1838 by Mulder's associate Jöns Jakob Berzelius; protein is derived from the Greek word (*proteios*), meaning 'primary', 'in the lead', or 'standing in front'. Mulder went on to identify the products of protein degradation such as the amino acid leucine for which he found a (nearly correct) molecular weight of 131 Da.

The difficulty in purifying proteins in large quantities made them very difficult for early protein biochemists to study. Hence, early studies focused on proteins that could be purified in large quantities, e.g., those of blood, egg white, various toxins, and digestive/metabolic enzymes obtained from slaughterhouses. In the 1950s, the Armour Hot Dog Co. purified 1 kg of pure bovine pancreatic ribonuclease A and made it freely available to scientists; this gesture helped ribonuclease A become a major target for biochemical study for the following decades.

Linus Pauling is credited with the successful prediction of regular protein secondary structures based on hydrogen bonding, an idea first put forth by William Astbury in 1933. Later work by Walter Kauzmann on denaturation based partly on previous studies by Kaj Linderstrøm-Lang, contributed an understanding of protein folding and structure mediated by hydrophobic interactions. In 1949 Fred Sanger correctly determined the amino acid sequence of insulin, thus conclusively demonstrating that proteins consisted of linear polymers of amino acids rather than branched chains, colloids, or cyclols. The first atomic-resolution structures of proteins were solved by X-ray crystallography in the 1960s and by NMR in the 1980s. As of 2009, the Protein Data Bank has over 55,000 atomic-resolution structures of proteins. In more recent times, cryo-electron microscopy of large macromolecular assemblies and computational protein structure prediction of small protein domains are two methods approaching atomic resolution.

12

# India's Traditional Dairy Products

From burfi to kulfi, from *kalakand* to *shrikhand*, from *gulabjamun* to *chumchum* extends the delectable world of Indian milk delicacies.This article brings together information culled from diverse sources on age-old, milk-based specialties from different regions. Also included is information culled from diverse sources on the Indian milk-based sweets and other specialties from different regions of the country.

Since time immemorial, a significant proportion of milk has been used in India for preparing a wide variety of dairy delicacies — an unending array of sweets and other specialties from different regions of the country. In the process, the basic limitation of milk — its perishable nature — has been tastefully overcome. Its processing aims to extend the shelf-life of milk, while converting it into mouth-watering tit-bits. Thus, diverse methods to prepare as well as preserve milk products have been developed. An estimated 50 to 55 per cent of the milk produced in India is converted into a variety of traditional milk products, using processes such as coagulation (heat and/or acid), desiccation and fermentation. Over the millennia, these processes have largely remained unchanged, being in the hands of halwais, the traditional sweetmeat makers, who form the core of this cottage industry. Although 46 per cent of the milk produced in the country is consumed as liquid milk, increase in consumption can be stimulated. Milk plays an important role in the national diet. In Indian households, the life of milk is extended from 12 to 24 hours by repeated boiling. It is preserved by souring with the aid of lactic cultures, which imparts an acid taste, particularly refreshing in hot climate.

## Curd

The first of these products developed was *dahi* (curds or yogurt), obtained by fermenting milk. In the process, the digestibility of milk constituents improves.The product is widely consumed along with meals. The surplus dahi is used as the intermediate product and churned into *makkhan* (butter), while the liquid whey — *chhach* or *mattha* — is consumed as a refreshing beverage or converted into *kadhi*, a spicy dish served hot with rice.

*Nutritional benefits:* When food is supplemented with 250 gms of dahi a day, the status of thiamine improves. *Dahi* also increases the pyruvic and lactic acids among children on a typical poor rice diet. Due to fermentation of milk, a greater amount of phosphorus and calcium is made available to the digestive system by their precipitation in the lower intestines due to the acid condition induced by Lactobacillus sp. The consumption of sour milk also results in increased efficiency of the human body to cope with a sudden influx of lactic acid in the system. Dahi can also be consumed by people who suffer from lactose intolerance. Thus, dahi in its different forms as lassi, kadhi, shrikhand, etc. also contributes significantly to improve the nutritive contents of an average Indian diet.

## Ghee and Makkhan

A week's collection of makkhan (butter) is converted into *ghee*. *Dahi* has a shelf-life of a day or two; *makkhan*, a week; and *ghee*, about a year. Ghee, thus, became the main dairy product for extended preservation. A system of collection of ghee from villages for trade gradually developed. Ghee mandis (trading centers) have been in existence for centuries. India produces some 9,00,000 tonnes of *ghee*, valued at ₹ 85,000 million.The value of the resultant *lassi* is ₹ 25,000 million.

For most uses, the wholesome flavor of *ghee* is its chief attraction. For table use, it is served in melted form and mixed with rice or lightly spread on *chappatis*. It is widely used for shallow frying and deep frying of food. Innumerable Indian sweetmeats based on cereals, milk solids, fruits and vegetables are cooked, by preference, in ghee.

Butter-milk is a by-product in the preparation of *makkhan*. It is estimated that about 55 kg of butter-milk is produced for every kg of ghee. While most of it is consumed by villagers and their families, some quantity is either given away or fed to cattle. The reason for this is lack of any market for it in rural areas. Butter-milk is rich in milk protein and calcium, and forms a nutritive and refreshing beverage.

*Nutritional benefits:* Makkhan and ghee contribute as much as one-third of the fat in the Indian diet. Ghee is produced mainly for consumption directly as food and as an ingredient of food preparations including sweets. Over the centuries, people have cultivated a liking for the aroma and flavor of ghee and prefer it over vegetable oils, the other traditional cooking medium. The vegetarian habits of many Indians preclude from their diet animal fats such as tallow or lard, used in the West. Thus, ghee forms an important source of fat in the vegetarian diet. *Ghee* and *makkhan* are important sources of vitamins A, D, E and K. They also contain small amounts of essential fatty acids such as arachidonic and linoleic. Considerable losses of Vitamin A and carotene can occur during cooking, the latter being more rapid. Below 125 °C, Vitamin A is fairly stable, but above this temperature it is rapidly destroyed. Some 10-20 per cent of carotene is lost during the normal cooking operations.

## Khoa and Chhana

One major milk product in common use is *khoa*, obtained by rapidly evaporating milk in shallow pans to a total solids of about 70 per cent and capable of being preserved as such for several days. It is used as an ingredient in making different kinds of traditional mithais (sweets) such as *peda*, *burfi* and *gulabjamun*. Some 900,000 tonnes of khoa valued at ₹ 45,000 million is produced in the country.

Yet another milk product of significance is *chhana*, a product of acid coagulation of hot milk and draining out of whey. It is used in preparing different kinds of sweets such as rasagollas. As they are especially popular in the Eastern region, they are called Bengali sweets. Approximately 12,00,000 tonnes of chhana, valued at ₹ 6,000 million is produced in India.

The value of khoa and chhana produced is probably twice the value of all milk handled by the organized sector in the country. The traditional dairy products sector in India, like its agricultural counterpart, is grossly undermanaged. It, however, provides economic opportunities that even the Western dairy world would be envious of. The value of khoa and chhana-based sweets could possibly exceed ₹ 1,30,000 million.

India's high-value, high-volume market for traditional dairy products and delicacies is all set to boom further under the technology of mass production. This market is the largest in value after liquid milk and is estimated at US $3 billion in India and US $1 billion overseas.

More and more dairy plants in the public, cooperative and private sectors in India are going in for the manufacture of traditional milk products. This trend will undoubtedly give a further stimulus to the milk consumption in the country and ensure a better price to primary milk producers. Simultaneously, it will also help to productively utilize India's growing milk surplus.

## LIST OF CHEESES

This is a list of cheeses by place of origin.

### Africa

#### *Egypt*

- Sardo cheese
- Testouri cheese

#### Ethiopia

- Ayib cheese

#### Mauritania

- Caravane cheese

#### South Africa

- Bokmakiri cheese
- Kwaito cheese

### Asia

#### China

- Rubing
- Rushan
- Nguri

#### Georgia

- Suluguni

#### India

- Paneer
- Chhena
- Khoa (food)

#### Bangladesh

- Chhena

**Japan**

- Sakura cheese

**Middle East**

- Labneh
- Ackawi
- Basket cheese
- Jameed
- Jibneh Arabieh
- Kenafa
- Nabulsi
- Paneer
- Shanklish
- Syrian cheese

**Nepal**

- Flower of Rajya

**Philippines**

- Kesong or Quesong Puti

**Tibet**

- Chura kampo
- Chhurpi

**Europe**

***Austria***

- Bergkäse
- Brimsen (Austrian term for Bryndza)
- Lüneberg cheese
- Tyrolean grey cheese
- Montafoner Sauerkäse

- Tiroler Graukäse
- Mondseer
- Gelundener Käse
- Bachensteiner
- Staazer
- Steirerkäse

**Belgium**

- Limburger cheese
- Affligem
- Bruges Gold
- Brussels cheese
- Chimay
- Damme
- Damme brie
- Herve cheese

Limburger cheese, a soft white cheese with a very strong odour and flavour.

- Mandjeskaas
- Maredsous cheese
- Passendale cheese
- Remedou cheese
- Rochefort cheese
- Rodoric cheese

**Bulgaria**

- Kashkaval
- Sirene
- Katyk
- Izvara
- Dunavia

**Cyprus**

- Grilled Halloumi (Cyprus)
- Anari
- Halloumi (Hellim)
- Kefalotyri

**Croatia**

- Paski sir (Pag Island cheese)
- Skripavac ('Squeaking' cheese from Lika)
- Tounjski sir (Smoked cheese from Tounj near Ogulin)
- Dimsi (Smoked cheese from Zagreb based on Bjelovarac cheese)

**Czech Republic**

- Olomoucké syrecky

**Denmark**

- Danish Blue cheese
- Danbo
- Danish Blue cheese (*Dansk blåskimmel(ost)*)
- Danish tilsit or *Tilsit Havarti*
- Esrom or *Danish Port-Salut*
- Havarti cheese or *Cream Havarti*
- Saga cheese

**Finland**

- Aura
- Lappi cheese
- Leipäjuusto ('bread-like cheese', i.e. oven-baked cheese)
- Oltermanni
- Raejuusto (*Finnish cottage cheese*)

**France**

- Selles-sur-cher cheese

See the French AOC cheeses and the list of French cheeses

**Germany**

- Bavaria blu
- Bonifaz

Cambozola, a combination of French Camembert and Italian Gorgonzola.

- Harzer cheese
- Handkäse
- Hirtenkäse
- Limburger cheese
- Romadur
- Milbenkäse
- Rauchkäse
- Tilsit cheese
- Weisslacker

**Greece**

- Formaela
- Anthotyros
- Arseniko Naxou - (Naxos)
- Batzos, PDO
- Chèvre Metsovou - (Metsovo)
- Feta, PDO - ( Epirus, Macedonia, Thrace, Thessaly, Peloponnese)
- Formaela, PDO - Arachova)
- Froumaela Valmandouras Peloponnese)
- Galotyri, PDO - Thessaly, Epirus)
- Graviera, PDO - Agrafa, Crete, Naxos

- Kalathaki
- Kalathotos
- Karikeftos
- Kaseri, PDO — Macedonia, Thrace, Thessaly)
- Katiki, PDO — Domokos)
- Kefalograviera, PDO — Crete, Sterea Ellada)
- Kefalotyri
- Kopanisti, PDO — Mykonos)
- Krasotyri — (Kos)
- Ladenios
- Ladotyri, PDO — Lesvos)
- Malaka
- Manouri
- Mastelo
- Manoura Sifnou
- Melichloro
- Metsovella
- Metsovone
- Myzithra
- Petroti
- Pichtogalo Chanion
- San Michali
- Sfela
- Stamatini
- Touloumisio
- Xygalo
- Xynomizithra Myconos
- Xynotyro

**Hungary**

A serving of Liptauer

- Liptauer
- Trappista cheese
- Pálpusztai
- Pannónia

**Iceland**

- Höfðingi
- Skyr

**Ireland**

- Gubbeen cheese
- Ardrahan cheese
- Cashel Blue cheese
- Coolea cheese
- Corleggy cheese
- Dubliner cheese
- Durrus Cheese
- Gubbeen cheese

**Netherlands**

- Edam
- Gouda
- Leerdammer
- Limburger cheese
- Leyden cheese
- Maasdam
- Parrano
- Roomano
- Vlaskaas

**Macedonia**

- Sirenje
- Kashkaval
- Urda

**Malta and Gozo**

- Gbejna (*Gbejna*)

**Norway**

- Brunost
- Gamalost
- Geitost
- Gudbrandsdalsost
- Jarlsberg
- Nøkkelost
- Norvegia
- Pultost
- Snøfrisk

**Poland**

- Twaróg
- Bryndza
- Bundz
- Bursztyn — mature cheese similar to Gruyere
- Golka
- Korycinski
- Oscypek
- Redykolka
- Rokpol
- Twaróg also known as Quark (cheese)
- Tylzycki — semi-hard, yellow cheese made from cow's milk

**Portugal**

- Castelo Branco
- Requeijão
- Saloio
- Santarém
- São Jorge
- Serra da Estrela
- Tomar

**Brânza de burduf**

- Brânza topita
- Cascaval
- Cas
- Urda
- Telemea

**Russia**

Tvorok a curd cheese as in cheesecake, somewhat similar to cottage cheese or Ricotta.

Rossiyski cheese, similar to German Tilsiter.

**Serbia**

- Kackavalj
- Sremski

**Slovakia**

- Bryndza
- Liptauer
- Korbaciky
- Otiepok
- Parenica
- Tvaroh

**Spain**

- Manchego cheese
- Afuega'l pitu
- Cabrales cheese
- Garrotxa cheese
- Idiazabal cheese
- Mahón cheese
- Majorero cheese
- Manchego cheese
- Mató cheese (Catalonia)
- La Serena cheese (Extremadura)
- Picón Bejes-Tresviso
- Tetilla cheese
- Torta del Casar
- Valdeón
- Zamorano cheese

**Sweden**

- Swedish Herrgårdsost
- Blå Gotland (*Gotland Blue*)
- Grevé
- Herrgårdsost
- Hushållsost
- Prästost
- Svecia
- Västerbottensost

**Turkey**

- Beyaz peynir
- Çökelek

- Dil peyniri
- Ezine peyniri
- Edirne peyniri
- Kasar peyniri
- Keçi peyniri
- Küp peyniri
- Otlu peynir
- Örgü peynir
- Telli peynir
- Tulum peyniri

**Canada**

- Amster Dammer (British Columbia)
- Balderson's Cheddar (Ontario)
- Baron (Quebec)
- Bleu Bénédictin (Quebec)
- Bleu L'Ermite (Quebec)
- Bleubry (Quebec)
- Bocconcini (Ontario)
- Bouq Emissaire (Quebec)
- Brie Manoir (Quebec)
- Brie L'extra Double Crème (Quebec)
- Brie Vaudreuil (Quebec)
- Brie Chevalier Fines Herbes (Quebec)
- Brittania (Quebec)
- Camembert de Madame Clément (Quebec)
- Cantonnier (Quebec)
- Cheddar âgé au Porto 10 ans (Quebec)
- Chèvre noir (Quebec)

- Damablanc (Quebec)
- Douanier, Le (Quebec)
- Dragon's Breath Blue (Nova Scotia)
- Fétard (Quebec)
- Frère Jacques (Quebec)
- Friulano
- Gouda Coureur des Bois (Quebec)
- Gouda Old (British Columbia)
- Gouda Old Cheese (Ontario)
- Kingsberg (Quebec) Leoni-Grana Parmesan (Alberta) Mamirolle (Quebec) Medium Cheddar (Nova Scotia) Miranda (Quebec) Mont Saint-Benoît (Quebec) Mozzarella Yellow Prestigio(Quebec) Noyan (Quebec) Oka (Quebec) Pied-de-Vent (Quebec) Provolone Sette Fette (Ontario) Raclette des Appalaches (Quebec) Raclette Fritz (Quebec) Raclette Griffon (Quebec) Riopelle de l'Isle, Le (Quebec) Saint-Fidèle (Quebec) Saint-Paulin Québécois (Quebec) Saint-Paulin Anco (Quebec) Smoked Monterey Jack (Manitoba) Tomme Québécoise (Quebec) Trevisano (Ontario) Valbert (Quebec) Verdelait Cracked Pepper (British Columbia) Victor et Berthold (Quebec)

**El Salvador**

- Cuajada
- Crema
- Fresco
- Enredo
- Queto

**Mexico**

- Oaxaca cheese
- Añejo (aged)

- Blanco (white)
- Chihuahua
- Cotija
- Criollo (Creole)
- Chiapas cheese
- Fresco (fresh)
- Oaxaca
- Panela
- Quesillo
- Requesón

**Nicaragua**

- Quesillo

**Oceania**

***Australia***

- Coon

**New Zealand**

- Chesdale
- Evansdale

**South America**

**Argentina**

- Reggianito
- Sardo

**Brazil**

- Coalho
- Catupiry
- Minas (a. k. a. 'Queijo Minas Padrão', 'Queijo Frescal' and 'Queijo Curado')

- Coalho
- Requeijão
- Prato

**Chile**

- A typical cut of Chanco cheese
- Chanco
- Gauda
- Panquehue
- Renaico

**Colombia**

- Quesillo

**Venezuela**

- Queso Guayanés
- Queso Palmita
- Queso de año
- Queso semiduro
- Queso crineja

# Index

## D

**E**



**F**



**G**

## M



## N